CALLED INTO DARKNESS

CHRIS DEFLORIO

Copyright © CHRIS DEFLORIO 2024
ALL RIGHTS RESERVED

No part of this book may be reproduced in any form
without permission from the author or publisher
except as permitted by US copyright law.
To request permission contact chrisdeflorio777@gmail.com

Cover Design by Annette Munnich Stellium Books
All photos courtesy of the author.

ISBN: 979-8-218-42115-1
FIRST EDITION

Stellium Books / Manufactured in the USA

DEDICATION

To my lovely wife, Harmony, my beautiful daughters, Sarah, Rebecca, and Samantha and to my amazing son, Jake. You have all sacrificed so much over the past 15 years for me to live out my calling. I am truly a blessed husband and father to be surrounded by your love and support.

This book is dedicated to you. I love you all.

FOREWORD

It has often been said that the greatest lie the devil has ever told is that he doesn't exist. The devil is pictured like in the old Tom and Jerry cartoon that he is some guy in a red suit with a pitchfork. In fact, the Bible says that he disguises himself as an angel of light. There are many who have fallen for the lie that he doesn't exist or that he is some harmless religious superstition. They have reaped a whirlwind of trouble for themselves.

Witchcraft is on the rise in America. People are experimenting with Ouija boards, calling on the dead, palm reading, fortune telling etc. As a result, without even knowing it, they have invited demons (fallen angels) into their lives and into their homes. There is a whole spiritual realm around us that most are unaware of. Spiritual warfare is real and there are many casualties.

Enter Chris and Harmony DeFlorio. I have known Chris and Harmony since 2011 when we started attending the same Church. At the time, Chris was an NYPD Officer. In my initial conversations with Chris, I was very impressed with his Biblical knowledge and even more so his heart for evangelism.

Chris has been misunderstood. I have been a follower of Jesus Christ for 25 years. There have been a few people that I have come across that have an absolute passion to share the Gospel of Jesus Christ with those who do not know. Chris DeFlorio is one of those people.

I have seen Chris go to foreign countries, go on the streets of New York City, and the local streets of Long Island to let people know that there is a God who loves them.

Chris DeFlorio has done extensive research in the area of Demonology. He has been diligently studying this topic for years. He also has firsthand knowledge of this subject as he has encountered the demons he has studied. The ministry of Chris and Harmony DeFlorio is based on extensive knowledge, hands on experience and a love for people who are trapped in demonic oppression.

Chris and Harmony are now involved in the ministry of setting people free from the grip of Satan. They are not chasing ghosts. They are confronting demons face to face in order to set people free. Their journey is an amazing one and it is not over; it is just beginning.

Tom Strigaro
Senior Pastor
Lift Jesus Higher Fellowship
Farmingville, NY

PREFACE

I have been told many times over the past five years that our story belongs in a book. Until now, I never felt the time was right. As I began to recount the story of our supernatural cases together and how Harmony and I ended up here, I began to see that there were actually two stories working together. A book that would not just showcase to the world the unbelievable supernatural events of our cases as they open another world to readers that they may have never seen before. But also, a book that could help others understand their place in this world.

It has been said that the work that my wife and I do is very dangerous and should not be attempted by anyone. It may surprise you that those comments predominantly came from Christians. Many of the misconceptions and misunderstandings of what we do have been from the area of the Church. It was also for these reasons why this book was written. Not as a rebuke but to educate.

On the one hand, people who say it is dangerous to attempt are correct in some way. I have tried my best to show through our story how this was not something we chose but this path was chosen for us. I encourage you to be mindful to read all the events as a whole and not as separate events. So many times, in life, we never truly understand the path that has been laid out for each one of us until we look back in hindsight.

The book will showcase the Connecticut case that was in the news as I will share the entire story that has never been told before. The reader will experience the step-by-step process that we went through from the initial call to the final confrontation as you will experience the emotional rollercoaster right alongside us. Along the way, you will read of some other amazing cases and events that we encountered that helped shape the way we do ministry.

I will also attempt to show the reader the Divine path that God had laid out for Harmony and me individually. You will have a front row seat as you witness the evolution from two lost souls to soldiers for God. I will attempt to show how we were being equipped while living in both worlds of the physical and spiritual to enter this war.

Through the telling of the two stories, I will focus on three main points. Evangelism, God's divine path, and real attacks of the devil and his demons.

This is and always was a ministry of evangelism. We are not ghost hunters, or crazy Christians yelling yahoo as we run into homes to fight the devil. The first century ministry of casting out demons was performed by Christians as an advancement of the Gospel. It was to show that Christ was the Messiah, the power of God and that the New Covenant in Christ was at hand. I warn anyone who attempts to work in this ministry, that if the Gospel is not the center of your involvement, you are missing the point. Harmony and I have been involved in evangelistic events all over the world and I always tell people, this is the easiest ministry I have ever been involved in. In no other area of ministry have I had people invite me into their home and say, "Please help me, what must I do to be saved?"

Harmony and I lived remarkably interesting lives as a police officer and medic, husband and wife, dad, and mom as Christian believers. Through our journey in the NYPD and FDNY, we have developed many tools of the trade that have equipped us specifically to perform in this ministry. We have been walking into complete strangers' homes to help them in their worst worldly moments for over twenty years as first responders. Using this skill alone, God has prepared us to be used as first responders to enter homes and help those suffering in the spiritual realm as well. This ministry is something you must be equipped to do.

Also, I have had many years of study in Theology and Spiritual Warfare, while putting it into action on the streets. I cannot emphasize enough that without Biblical understanding combined with knowledge of the enemy, you should not jump into this work. It requires a lot more than repeating a scripture. I received many calls from people attempting this ministry without the proper Biblical context and have gotten themselves or their family into bad situations.

I would also like to clear something up. Reading a name in a book or looking at a picture will not hurt you or open a spiritual door. These are called myths and superstitions. It is a matter of your heart and your intent that will get you in trouble. There is a major difference between curiosity and education. Education is priceless and necessary to be able to survive if you choose to enter the spiritual war.

I never imagined this for my life or even thought about this other world. Once you enter this world where you not only see the demonic, but they also see you as well. There is no turning back. You and your family will be on the radar of the enemy as you are taking an active part in setting people free. There will be consequences, so unless you are ready to never look back to your regular life, think again.

Last but certainly not least, we are doing this because people are in trouble. We have always tried to follow the two greatest commandments, to love God and love neighbor. I will admit I have never kept either one perfectly as many can attest to, but I will never stop moving forward.

There have been many opinions, rumors and gossip towards my wife and I that hurt us very much from people we knew for many years. At one point, we began to doubt our calling.

Not too long after, we did a televised interview with a famous Christian host. Almost immediately, I received over 5,000 calls for help in less than two months. So many, that I almost needed counseling for myself to process the wide range of demonic attacks going on in the lives of so many families. Surprisingly, most were turned away from pastors or could not get in touch with exorcists.

My wife and I made the decision to never turn from what God has called us to do because of the opinions of man. The truth is that the Devil is real, and families are being held hostage by the demonic because they are afraid to speak up at the risk of public ridicule. Whether someone is a Christian, atheist, or follower of any religion, we will be there to help these people. We will fight for them and be their voice as we continue to be ministers of the Gospel, going out **two by two**, just as God has always sent us.

I would like to acknowledge a few people who have been indispensable in my life and ministry.

I am forever grateful to my wife and partner in ministry, Harmony, you have been my greatest supporter in everything I have ever embarked on. You have been my strength as you have never let me throw in the towel when things got tough. It has always been Chris and Harmony. You are my life and best friend. I love you.

To my children, although you may have hidden your face at the ridicule of your parents (That was a joke) you have always stood by us. Either by having me speak at college classes or sending us to your friends to help, you encouraged both mom and I in ways you never understood. We are forever thankful for your love and support as a family.

To Stephen Doucette and Pastor Tom Strigaro. You guys have been our most faithful friends. Friends that we could always depend on when the doubters came or when we were abandoned at times. You are both examples of unconditional love and men of true faith. Without either of you, I could not have continued in this ministry.

A special thanks to my Publicist, Breanna Walther of Suden PR. You have been invaluable to me, not only as a publicist but also a friend.

The events contained in this book, as unbelievable as they may seem, are all true. They can be verified by eyewitnesses, video, photo or audio recordings. Some names, genders and locations have been changed to honor requests to protect confidentiality.

Also, I have chosen to write this story from an outside perspective to create a story type atmosphere for the reader to enjoy as you might with a novel.

I will not provide formal teaching on Demonology or the occult in this book. It is not intended to be a book of expertise, but a true story of two people called to take on the devil in our realm. If you observe how I perform certain techniques and tactics during a case, you will learn a thing or two. The teaching will be in the details of the story.

My prayer for each one of you reading this book is for you to discover in your own lives, the path and direction God has called you to. Follow it. Embrace it. As you go, never forget, Glorify God and love your neighbor. These are the two most important things to remember wherever HE takes you.

Finally, I will leave it up to the reader to decide if we are qualified for this ministry. My hope is that after reading the entire story and processing the evidence, I have presented a clear picture for you to decide in either direction. Are we unfit to help those who are out of the reach of the Churches? Or were we brought into the light to join this battle and...CALLED into DARKNESS to seek and save the lost... Enjoy the ride.

Chris DeFlorio
Ronkonkoma, NY

TABLE OF CONTENTS

CONNECTICUT- MAY 2021	1
A DIVINE MEETING	5
CONNECTICUT-THE BEGINNING	19
THE SKY BECAME DARK	39
CONNECTICUT- THE COP & THE CAREGIVER	57
THE RETURN TO OZ	75
CONNECTICUT- MARBAS & THE CHILD	93
THE SKY NEVER LOOKED SO BLUE	125
SPIRITUAL WARFARE BEGINS	135
CONNECTICUT- THE DEVIL INSIDE	153
MINISTRY 2009-2018	173
OUT OF AFRICA	185
A HAUNTED VACATION	201
LEAVING FLORIDA	227
CONNECTICUT – THE CONFRONTATION	239

CHAPTER ONE

CONNECTICUT
May 2021

The smoke from the burning frankincense filled the air as Chris paced anxiously back and forth through the dimly lit, unfinished, attic. The sunny spring afternoon which was filled with brightness and slow-moving translucent clouds gave way to eerie darkness as the storm rolled in. The peaceful sound of chirping birds quickly turned to sharp rain drops bouncing off the roof directly above their heads.

With his head down, he read from an old leather book. He glanced across the room while he continued to read aloud in the original language of the New Testament. Harmony stood only a few feet away on the opposite end of the attic. There was only a small surface area of wooden planks covering the floor studs amid the unwalkable attic. She stood alert holding a large wooden cross in her hands. She was not taking her focus off her husband. She knew her role as she would be his only eyes and ears for his safety.

He continued to read, "Ἐν ἀρχῇ ἦν ὁ Λόγος, καὶ ὁ Λόγος ἦν πρὸς τὸν Θεόν, καὶ Θεὸς ἦν ὁ Λόγος."

Translation: John 1:1 In the beginning was the Word: The Word was with God ***and the Word was God.***
Suddenly, the smell of what can only be described as feces filled the room. A smell so pungent, it was as if it was purposely attempting to replace the glorious smell of

the frankincense. Chris was now having difficulty continuing the prayer. He started to choke up from the smell as it moved to his eyes, and they began to burn. The battle was now tangible.

Seconds, later Harmony cried out, "There is something behind me!"

Chris stopped what he was doing and raced towards Harmony. Holy water splashed over the walls behind her as he tossed it blindly into the distance.

The husband-and-wife team began the LORD'S PRAYER in unity and with command;

"Our Father, who art in Heaven, Hallowed be Thy name…"

Chris heard a strange sound. He threw his head up and quickly looked around as Harmony continued in the prayer.

Strange sounds began to fill the attic as it attempted to drown out the prayers.

Then just as quickly as the mysterious noise began, it vanished as the room went silent. With sweat sliding down their faces while catching their breaths, Chris and Harmony just looked at each other in disbelief at what had just occurred.

As Chris opened his mouth to read, He spoke the first word and suddenly from behind Harmony came…

ROAR!

CONNECTICUT MAY 2021

Chris threw his head up quickly. He knew exactly who and what that was. They had been tracking him for weeks. There was no doubt now it was him. Fear gripped the couple for as they could see they were outmatched. They knew the one that needed to show up. They needed to depend on their faith.

This was no worldly battle. This was a place where size and stature are insignificant, but only faith in the one true God, as this battle was not against flesh and blood but the kingdom of darkness, the Devil himself. Chris and Harmony DeFlorio were now taking part in a raging war that has been going on between God and the Devil since creation.

Chris stopped what he was doing as if time froze around him. He saw once again all that had transpired over the past 13 years leading to this moment. Just like in Florida, they were not some random people in the wrong place at the wrong time. No, they were being prepared for this one moment, their entire lives. It was here that he would flashback through time as if in that split second between leaving the physical and entering the invisible world, he could clearly see the steps God had laid out for both of them throughout their lives.

Chris with a face ready for war, looked at Harmony and said, "Here we go."

CONNECTICUT MAY 2021

CHAPTER TWO

A DIVINE MEETING

13 years earlier around 2008, Chris was entering his 5th year as a police officer at the New York City Police Departments (NYPD) 32nd Precinct located in Harlem. The 32nd Precinct had a reputation for being one of the busiest and most violent areas in all of New York city. It was a place most police officers would avoid at all costs. Rookies would use up favors for transfers as they would leave just as fast as they had arrived.

That was not the case with Chris, who was remarkably familiar with the area. He was running the streets as a paramedic for the New York City Fire Department in the same precinct area only months before. He was a creature of habit, so it made sense to him to stay where he was comfortable.

He remembered the day the Academy Sergeant was giving out the precinct assignments that they would report to. Chris was the Assistant Company Sergeant. This usually meant that he would have a good chance to pick a good command. As the Sergeant looked at Chris's precinct he paused.

He looked up and spoke, "Whose feet did you step on? You're going to the 32."

A DIVINE MEETING

As the group began to laugh, he realized no one knew he picked the unfavored precinct and he kept it that way.

After a few years on patrol, Chris was handpicked with a few others for the newly formed "Plain Clothes" Conditions Unit. Chris and the other police officer's assignment was to "attempt" to blend in on the busy Harlem streets. Attempt because every one of them looked like a fish out of water in their camo cargo shorts, T-shirts with funny logos and baseball caps. They were there to clean up the neighborhood of crimes that could potentially turn violent.

Chris loved this type of police work because it was here, he first learned one of the most important skills he would ever need. How to study human behavior. The art of observing movements and facial expressions that could tip one off to something as simple as a lie or as serious as a major crime that was about to take place. Skills he would need later in life as his work would one day take him to the most dangerous situations imaginable. The senior cops he worked with were full of wisdom and knowledge from years of dealing with this type of police work. This was where he would really learn the "streets."

Many times, one of the officers would spot a perpetrator (perp) carrying an illegal firearm. Foot pursuits became pretty routine during the overnight tours in the summer as you would hear over the radio, "Foot pursuit… man with a gun." The Anti-Crime Unit (another plain clothes unit) would work parallel to Chris's unit. Their objective was to focus on taking guns off the street.

It was common for Chris to be called up to this unit on a busy night to fill in for a vacancy. This was the case on

A DIVINE MEETING

a fateful Saturday night in August 2008 that would introduce Chris to his new partner. She would not be a partner in the police department but a future partner for a job neither of them even knew existed at the time.

Chris was sitting in the back of the black, unmarked, Crown Vic. This was the standard NYPD car for these units. Unmarked meaning they had no visible lights or symbols alerting potential perps of a police presence. What a joke, considering after one or two days after the car is introduced into circulation, everyone in the entire precinct area could recognize it was a police vehicle but that is a whole different story.

As they were cruising around and observing the busy nightlife of Harlem, groups of people could be seen on every corner. Grills lined the sidewalks as double-parked cars packed the side streets. Families sat in folding chairs, laughing as they ate and drank as if it was 2'o clock on a Sunday afternoon. But it wasn't, it was 1am which meant other activity was going on as well. The 32nd Precinct was known for its many shootings, stabbings, robberies, murders, you name it. The list could go on and on.

Many times, these were usually the result of the large crowds which gathered in the sweltering summer heat. Groups could be seen playing dice in the alleyways, hand-to-hand drug deals happening around parked cars, or the common gang-related issues in the area, were always a concern. But inside the car, with the windows up, the night could still feel peaceful on some level as they cruised through the dark of night.

A DIVINE MEETING

Suddenly, over the radio, a broken transmission as if someone were trying to speak. They all knew what was coming next.

An out of breath cop in a full sprint sending over a transmission, "Foot pursuit... Man... Gun... Male... black... red shirt... black shorts..."

That's all they needed to hear. Every precinct, sector and cop stopped what they were doing to listen for the location to help their brother or sister.

The adrenaline filled cop yelled, "Eastbound 129, 7th to Lenox."

Chris's unit began to race to the area. Running red lights as if it were a speedway, as all the driver was concerned about was getting to the cop's location as fast as possible. Chris and the rest listened intently for updates on the radio. police sirens filled the air as they could be heard in every direction for a mile. It is something you would have to experience firsthand to really understand, going from a quiet conversation to what can only be compared to complete chaos in a split second.

As the black unmarked car raced close to the scene, they saw two men sprinting down the unlit sidewalk. Chris and the other cop in the backseat jumped out of the car and joined the pursuit on foot as the others in the car raced in front to cut off the perp. As the uniformed cop tackled the gun-wielding perpetrator, Chris and his crew helped restrain him and cuff him up.

As the perpetrator was brought back to the 32nd and processed by the arresting officer, Chris sat on top of a desk, towards the entrance of the precinct. Joking around with other officers, talking about what just played out in the streets. In this world of intense pressure that most people will never understand, the coping mechanism for many officers to process the dangerous events they are exposed to daily was to make light of what they just experienced. Can you imagine trying to seriously process in real time what most people view as entertainment on TV? It is not logical to expect so.

Chris first learned how to deal with these situations on the ambulance in the South Bronx during the late 90's. This was a time in NYC that violence and murders were at a peak. He was not only dealing with treating injuries from violent crimes but severe medical issues as well. Death by medical illness was very common. Processing cardiac arrests, one after the other, day after day, Adults and children was enough to drive anyone to drink. In this world of cold harsh reality, first responders need to find a way to survive or risk becoming victims themselves.

It's after 1 am at the busy Harlem Police Precinct. Police officers can be seen walking all around with paperwork in their hands or fingerprinting perps. The sound of criminals in the jail cells yelling for a phone call could be heard throughout the building.

At the same time, the Desk Sergeant could be heard yelling at officers every couple of minutes, "Let's get this guy finished and get him out of here!"

The Desk Sergeant was responsible for basically everyone who entered the precinct. The longer the perp was at the precinct, the longer overtime was being paid to a cop or a perp could cause an issue he didn't want to deal with. He wanted them out as fast as they came in and honestly who could blame him?

A DIVINE MEETING

Officer Jones approached the desk, "Hey Sarge, this guy says he doesn't feel well?"

"Call him a bus" (which is the word used for ambulance among cops) replied, the annoyed Sergeant.

As Chris is talking and laughing it up, he sees two New York City Fire Department (FDNY) emergency medical technicians or EMT's walking in the doors with their equipment. It's not uncommon for the fire department ambulance to come and treat sick prisoners as the prisoners were always looking for a way out of the cell.

Chris was instantly mesmerized by one of the medics as she walked by. She stood about 5'4 and was cute. Her wavy blonde hair and hazel eyes would have most of the men turning to watch her as she walked by. She grabbed Chris's attention right away. It was as if in his mind he had left the conversation he was having with the other cops and was now captive to her alone.

He quickly noticed how she walked with a certain swagger. Unlike lots of other women he knew, she walked with this type of confidence that drew him in. He had to devise a plan to start a conversation to seek her out. Chris wasn't too shy when it came to this type of game. He thought he wasn't too shabby himself... at least in his own mind.

Chris began to talk himself up in his own head. "I'm a cop, I'm in the plain clothes unit and we just brought in this guy with a gun. She's going to fall for me right away. Come on, this should be easy."

As she made a second pass, Chris decided to move forward, "Hey, how's it going?"

A DIVINE MEETING

Busy and without stopping, she gave a quick look and replied, "Hey."

Chris could see she wasn't interested in a conversation right now but wasn't ready to give up. Then it hit him! Of course, medic! He was a medic in her department at one time. He figured there was a good chance she was from his old EMS station in this precinct area and being a higher medical authority would impress her. Knowing that he only had a brief time left before she was gone, he moved in again and asked, "Do you come out of Station 16 down the block?"

She replied, "Yep" without looking, to give a clear sign that she wasn't interested.

Chris knew this obviously was not the first time she had been hit on and knew to have her guard up around these cops. He decided to wait until she and her partner had finished treating the prisoner. As she was putting her equipment away, he tried one last time. Chris walked over and asked, "Does Lt. Rizzo still work there? I was a medic there before I switched to P.D."

She looked up surprised and replied, "You? You were a medic?" Before Chris could reply, she finished packing up and gave the commonly known goodbye that is understood by first responders. "Be safe," she said, and walked out the precinct with her partner.

That was it in Chris's mind. She was not interested, and he was not one to continually chase down a woman who blew him off.

As Harmony and her partner were sitting out front in the ambulance finishing up paperwork, her partner, Lisa,

A DIVINE MEETING

began to inquire what that conversation was about inside the precinct. "Was that cop coming on to you in there?" Lisa asked, smiling at Harmony.

Just then Chris walked out in front of the building with some of the other cops in his unit as they waited for the rest to come out. It was time to get back to the streets. Harmony and Lisa, still in a discussion about Chris, were looking his way out front.

Harmony replied to Lisa's earlier question and nonchalantly said, "I guess so, he was ok. He was a medic over at our station years ago."

Lisa asked, "So, are you going to go out with him?"

Harmony responded, "Nah, I didn't even get his name."

Lisa looked over slowly and said, "He's easy on the eyes. You should give him a shot. I would."

Harmony shoots back quickly laughing, "I bet you would."

They both began to laugh as Harmony says, "Ok, let's see what he says." Harmony now stared at Chris, made solid eye contact with him and waved him around to her side of the ambulance.

Chris walked around to the passenger side where Harmony was sitting. As she rolled down the window, he could see that her partner quickly looked down at her phone with a smirk. He knew they were saying something about him as he walked over, and he knew she was obviously going to be listening.

A DIVINE MEETING

Harmony began the conversation, "So, you worked at my station?"

Chris smiled and replied, "Yes I did." They went on for a couple of minutes talking about who knew who and stories about the "job." He finally said, "I'm Chris, so what's your name?"

She replied, "Harmony."

Chris with a smirk looked at her and said, "Very cute, that's not your name." Chris thought she was still playing games and giving him a hard time.

All through her life she has been asked this type of question about her name or had some type of comment when people would hear it. She kind of knew it was coming. Harmony looked at Chris smiling, "It is."

Now her partner Lisa who was pretending to be minding her own business looked up and chimed in, "Yep, that's her name."

Chris responded, "Wow, that's a great name. So where do you live?"

Harmony replied, "Right here in Harlem."

Now Chris can't help feeling that she is pulling his chain. Harlem is predominately an African American area but not just that. It was rare to see a blonde-haired beauty from EMS living in the area that she worked, especially as violent an area as this. Most cops and EMS workers predominately lived either upstate or out on Long Island. Call it needing a mental break from the busy city but that was usually the case.

Chris answered sarcastically, "Get out of here. Now I know your full of it."

She responded. "I sure do. Been here for a few years now."

Chris was more curious about this woman then ever now. Her name was unique, she lived in a tough area. This just increased the curiosity and attraction he felt for Harmony. He wanted to know more about her story. "Would you want to go out sometime and maybe get something to eat?" he asked.

Harmony was now confronted with the question. Chris wasn't playing games anymore and she knew she had a choice to make. "Sure," she replied.

Chris smiled, "Great, what's your number, I'll give you a call." As Harmony finished telling Chris her number, her phone suddenly rang. It was Chris, right in front of her. Harmony looked at him surprised but then realized he was checking to see if the number was her real number. Chris said to Harmony with a cocky smile, "It's what I do."

Call it years of street sense as a cop and medic or a lifetime of disappointment in his personal life, Chris did not take things at face value anymore.

Harmony could see something in his eyes. He wasn't like the other guys that would try to pick her up on the job. Harmony knew there was something more to him, the same way he could know that about her.

She looked straight at Chris with a sensitivity she had hid from him in the earlier interactions and softly said, "You don't trust much, do you?"

A DIVINE MEETING

Chris was completely caught off guard by the comment. Inside he felt as if she touched a sensitive nerve and could see right through him. It was as if something was forming between two strangers from one small conversation. Was this simply a chance meeting or something divine outside of their understanding at the time?

Chris smiled at her. The tough guy act was over. There was something more genuine between the two of them now. As they began to slowly pull off the curb, Chris softly said, "I'll call you" and gently touched her arm.

They softly locked eyes and smiled as the ambulance drove off.

A week went by, and Chris had not yet called. He was waiting for the right time or was it that he was just too nervous. Finally, one Friday as he was finishing his shift around midnight, he decided to give her a call. He remembered from their conversation at the precinct that they work the same schedules. He slipped away to a quiet part of the locker room as many cops were changing to begin or end their shifts to leave.

As the phone began to ring a little part of him was hoping for voicemail but that wasn't happening tonight. "Hello?" Could be heard on the other end of the phone.

"Hey, Harmony? It's Chris DeFlorio, the cop from the 32."

"Oh, hi Chris," Harmony returned happily.

A DIVINE MEETING

As it turned out, she was just finishing up as well. Timing couldn't have been better. The two decided to head out to a 24-hour diner in Manhattan to get something to eat.

As Chris pulled up to Harmony's fire station, he was greeted by some old partners. They asked surprised, "Hey Chris, what are you doing here?"

"Aren't you lost?" one guy chuckled referring to him leaving them for the NYPD.

Chris, not really interested in divulging the truth that he's actually there to take one of their coworkers out, tried to change the subject. "What's up guys?" Chris responded nervously as he knew Harmony was about to come out. "What's new over here? Things look the same," he said.

One of the guys hanging in Chris's open window on the passenger door, was about to respond and got tapped on the shoulder. Harmony, as if not concerned about them, said, "Excuse me guys, my ride's here," and got into the car.

His old friends stared at him with a foolish smirk. They were not about to let Chris get off the hook that easily. As Harmony sat down, one of the men closed the door for her. As Chris was trying to pull away, they began to playfully tease the couple as parents would. "Now don't you two stay out too late. Have her home at a reasonable hour," they said one after the other.

The car drove off with the guys still shouting as Chris and Harmony kept watching and laughing. As it turned out, it was actually something they both appreciated in their own way to help break the ice.

A DIVINE MEETING

As they walked into the busy Midtown diner, the atmosphere was as you would expect on a summer night in New York City. Tables were filled with waitresses and bus boys running around to tend to customers. As Harmony and Chris got situated at a little table in the middle of the organized chaos, it didn't seem to bother them. They were both looking forward to this night and not to mention this atmosphere was part of their jobs. It was nothing new.

Chris could not wait for a juicy burger and a beer. After a long shift, there was nothing better in his mind.

As the waitress asked for their order, Harmony excitedly said, "Can I please have yogurt mixed with fruit?"

Chris' face dropped. He thought to himself, "Do I eat like an animal on the first date or fake it and eat healthy as well?"

"You sir?" the waitress asked.

Chris replied, "That sounds good, I'll try the same."

Harmony looked at Chris with a look of approval, as she shook her head. She had the feeling he was trying to impress her but didn't fully let on. She said, "Wow, that's not what I was expecting to hear."

As the waitress wrote down the orders, she turned to walk away. Chris, rethinking his choice, couldn't resist. He yelled for the waitress, "Bring me a beer with that."

Harmony looked at Chris with a little smile and said, "Hey, you gave it a shot."

A DIVINE MEETING

Chris with a wink replied, "I had to hold onto part of my manhood, at least on the first date."

They both laughed and knew it was going to be a special night. There is a part of us in our soul that yearns for that special mate. The person who can sense exactly what the other may be feeling without many words. The person who doesn't judge us but understands. This person may come along once in a lifetime and when they meet worlds can change in an instant as it was with Chris and Harmony.

The spark was there from their first meeting, and both were curious to see what else there could be. You can look at someone on the outside but sometimes what's inside is a total surprise and something you have been both looking for your whole life.

Chris and Harmony have been living separate lives, but they were about to find out how similar they really were and nothing about their fateful collision in the universe was accidental. They were on a journey from your everyday first responders in the busiest 911 system in the country to the first responders of supernatural events. They would soon learn they were going to be among those chosen to live in the duality of worlds.

CHAPTER THREE

CONNECTICUT
The Beginning

It was midnight on a peaceful spring night in April 2021 in the Long Island suburbs. Harmony was sound asleep on the couch as Chris was just finishing a movie. The four kids, now in their teens and twenties, basically needed a GPS to follow their whereabouts. Samantha was home asleep. Beckie and Jake were each out with their friends while Sarah was away at college.

As the movie finished, Chris reached over to gently wake Harmony and put her to bed. Just then, the call comes into his social media... "We need your help! My sister Glenda cares for her four year-old nephew with special needs and her new home is haunted!" Honestly, this was not a shocking moment for Chris working 911 over the past 25 years. The old peace to chaos. It just may have struck again in the lives of the DeFlorio's which was becoming a regular thing between raising teenagers, policing, and battling hellraising demons.

This was not the first time Chris had received a message like this, in fact, there were hundreds. As Chris was about to wake Harmony, pictures and videos popped up on his phone. This type of work had become so busy that he had to purchase a second cell phone just to keep all the traffic separate from his personal life. So, he figured he would take a quick look first before bed. As Chris opened the first videos, his attention drastically switched.

The first video was like out of a horror film. Three pretty blonde women walking around a spooky attic, rain bouncing off the roof, as they filmed a few strange symbols painted around the walls and floors. You couldn't make it up. As Chris studied these symbols which are known as "Sigils" in this type of work, he noticed one that was predominantly painted around the attic. It was a very eerie looking image. It looked like a stick figure of a man with crosses for arms with a circle surrounding him.

The next video revealed animal skulls nailed to the unfinished beams of the ceiling. Not far off, sat a circle of salt with wax residue from candles. Chris could see just from the videos that there was a great possibility that a conjuring ceremony was conducted in that room. Simply put, a conjuring ceremony would result in a person summoning a demonic entity from the spirit world directly into ours. Chris was concerned but still didn't see any evidence that any activity was even occurring in the home...Until he opened the next video.

The homeowner and victim, Glenda, filmed this video days earlier to send to her sisters for help. It's late at night, she is dressed in pajamas as if she had just woken up in some sort of distress. Glenda is seen walking around her home filming a type of selfie POV style video. She is frantic and on edge. The home looks beautifully furnished as she is seen walking around the second-floor narrating what she just experienced. She explains noises that were coming from a particular area of the ceiling, which would be the attic floor.

CONNECTICUT - THE BEGINNING

Suddenly, BANG...then footsteps...followed by what sounded like metal being torn apart.

Chris took a double take as he replayed the video repeatedly, attempting to debunk it. Chris thought to himself, "this is either some great hoax, or there is a rational explanation, or this woman is in trouble." Either way, he messaged the victim, Glenda, immediately and set up a phone interview for tomorrow.

The next day, Chris opened the door, turned on a dim light and walked into his office. He took a second to fire up his impressive workstation. As he pressed the power button to his computer, a total of four monitors began to turn on, one after the other. The dark room began to glow with a series of bluish, greenish lights as global tracking systems with digital maps and radars filled the screens. Programs that he had personally created through his own computer programmer.

As Chris prepared the call to Glenda, he opened pictures and videos related to Glenda's case to review, as he began to place them on the monitors.

He brought out his notepad as he knew this was not going to be a short interview. He was not going to miss any pertinent information. As the phone began to ring, He could only imagine the story that was about to unfold before him. He began to pray silently for wisdom and discernment to understand this situation correctly. To be able to debunk it promptly or to confirm it. To handle this alone or to know to call for backup from the Church.

As Chris waited intently for Glenda to answer, one thing he was not aware of was that he was about to begin a

CONNECTICUT - THE BEGINNING

case that in a few months' time was going to become a national news story.

Suddenly, he was jolted back to reality to the sound of, "Hi Chris, It's Glenda, thank you so much for calling."

Chris responded, "Hi Glenda, so I looked at your footage. What's been going on over there?"

As Glenda began to tell the story, he could tell right away from the language she spoke, the tempo of her voice and description of events, that she was of a sound mind and someone to take seriously what she believed she was seeing. One thing Chris learned as a medic and cop was to investigate the complainant as well as the crime itself. Now that this is a spiritual crime as he called it, and not a physical assailant, it would take a lot more attention to detail to diagnose. Glenda had seemed to pass the first test.

Before she could continue Chris interrupted and asked, "One thing I'm trying to understand about the markings in the attic. Didn't you see them before you moved in? Are you telling me, that the first time you saw them or entered the attic, was after the activity you filmed that night?"

Chris had a very detailed and methodical procedure when interviewing a complainant/victim or C/V. He asked many questions regarding the activity in the homes but what Chris was most concerned with was the people themselves. He wanted to know who he was dealing with on the other end of the phone.

As well as the pedigree information, he required any medical background history of the victim. Chris was a nationally registered paramedic in the past, so he

CONNECTICUT - THE BEGINNING

understood the importance of a person's mental state and history when taking a report. He also would be able to understand diagnoses and why certain medication would be administered to a victim. He would use these findings to help draw a rational conclusion of what may be happening to them.

On more than one occasion, Chris and Harmony had to refer a victim to a mental health facility. One case where a woman was having delusions that lined up with Schizophrenia. With this type of case, they would have to act quickly many times for the protection of the public as well as the victim.

Another time, Chris had to assist the FBI after he received a strange call for help from someone who said he could not control an urge to perform a mass shooting. The man said it was a demon telling him to do it, but then cut off communication with Chris. After working together, Chris was able to lead the FBI to the city and general location of the caller through social media.

Chris was prepared using interviewing techniques learned from his work as a police officer. He would ask a person to repeat certain events to be sure they lined up correctly or know when to dive deeper into a specific area.

Combined with the knowledge of Scripture and knowledge of the dark world of the occult, he was more than equipped. He helped anyone from any religion with any beliefs, suffering from possible diabolical issues. No one was turned away because of what they believed. Chris and Harmony made sure to meet people where they were at.

CONNECTICUT - THE BEGINNING

Glenda explained, "Actually I first moved in with my now ex-boyfriend. He is the one who cleaned it out at the time. The attic is very difficult to enter."

Chris followed up, "Did he say anything about the markings or animal skulls?"

She answered, "He said there is some wacky crap and that he threw out some garbage that was up there."

Chris asked with sarcasm towards the guy, "That's all this guy said? Garbage?"

She replied with a sigh, "That was his attitude towards everything and pretty much why he's not here anymore."

Chris knew it was time to change gears because that's one road he was not interested in going down right now. So let me ask you, "Do you attend Church or have a pastor or priest helping you?" He was never looking to replace a priest or pastor. Chris's motivation was to lead them back into the Church. One of his first questions was to always discover their faith or the Church's involvement. If they had one, he recommended going to their own leader. If they did not, he would offer to help find them a Church. The conundrum Chris and Harmony experienced often was that the multitudes of calls coming in desperately expressed that they couldn't find help in the Church.

As Glenda began to explain the situation, she explained they used to attend a Baptist Church as kids out in Oklahoma but not for a long time. She had many different views on organized religion and Chris could tell it was not a focus in her life.

CONNECTICUT - THE BEGINNING

She gave a summary of events that have been going on over the past few weeks. Alot of it, Chris could confirm from the videos that were sent to him from her sister. He was listening for consistency with her story right from the beginning.

The story that Glenda began to slowly sift through next was more than he was expecting.

She went on to say, "Well, it started about two weeks after moving in. Ms. Wilkins, the prior owner, showed up unannounced at the home asking to come in. She wanted to pick up items that she was not able to bring with her before they moved in. After I denied her access both times, she went on to plead with me to keep the neighbor off the one corner of her property. She kept saying, "It's not his property and he doesn't belong there."

Glenda continued, "She was abruptly evicted from the home and seemed dead set on getting back in. When I asked her to politely leave, her posture changed towards me and became agitated. I do remember, suddenly she began to stare at me with a weird smirk and walked out."

Chris commented, "Ok, so she didn't sell you the house, she was evicted. I'm sure that was something she was not happy about."

Glenda replied, "Exactly, in fact, the next day when I was taking my nephew, Tommy, to the bus stop, I found a very strange pile of sticks. The strange thing wasn't that there was a pile of sticks at the front of my driveway, but the pattern they made."

Chris quickly asked before she could move on, "Can you describe the pattern of sticks in the driveway?"

"Well, she said, I guess something with crosses and strange designs. I did take a picture if you would like to see it?"

Chris curiously replied, "Absolutely. Please send it over now so I can take a look and examine it."

As he was waiting, Glenda added, "At this point I decided to ask some neighbors about her. She was not well liked at all. She would cause problems with other neighbors."

She went on to say, "One neighbor explained that she would throw objects into the running brook that connected their backyards."

"Another said, she was a witch. Until now I just figured they meant she was mean." Chris and Glenda, trying to find some sort of small humor in this to maybe alleviate the severity of the situation, chuckled together at that comment.

As Glenda's picture of the sticks popped directly onto one of his computer monitors, something stuck out right away. He quickly began to flip through the media evidence he obtained from Glenda's sister. He knew there was a resemblance to something he saw before but what?

Chris leaned back into his chair as a feeling that can be described as a combination of awe and panic gripped him. He found the photo of the sigil in the attic. The one in the driveway was the same style as the one painted around the attic. Chris instantly knew how amazing this was to link the two activities. At the same time, he understood the magnitude of what was going on here. She's not just in

CONNECTICUT - THE BEGINNING

trouble with a spiritual assailant but quite possibly a physical one around her property as well.

As they began to summarize the events, Glenda added a shocking statement that put the case on a different level in the fraction of a second. "And what's troubling is that my nephew has a special name for this thing in the attic."

Chris taking a moment, asked, "he what?"

Glenda with a nervous chuckle, "Yes exactly. For some reason he calls it Shau or Meshaw. Tommy is special needs, and one issue is his speech. My brother is a widower and just received a new job in another country. He is over there now getting things situated with their home and new school for Tommy. I am caring for him until things are ready to try to help alleviate any unnecessary stress in his life."

Chris asked, "When did this begin?"

Glenda responded, "About a week ago."

Chris realized that the more he asked, the deeper this story was about to go. Things were adding up right away in a specific direction, a direction he was not thrilled with. As he continued to listen to Glenda describe the events, he did not let on to the severity of the situation that he felt was developing.

Chris ended the call without revealing much of his findings as he did not want to bring more fear to the situation before he arrived. He basically expressed some warnings to look for and directions for her to follow. Chris hung up the phone in a hurry and immediately sought out Harmony in the kitchen.

CONNECTICUT - THE BEGINNING

"Honey," he shouted, "I just spoke with the woman from this Connecticut case. It's looking much more serious than it even looked before the call."

Harmony responded with a look of surprise, "More serious than what you showed me in the videos?"

Chris and Harmony worked well on these cases together. He shared all the information he obtained in the initial stages of a case, as well as investigating scenes on location. Combining both their professional backgrounds and Christian faith, they were an effective team.

Chris, dropping his head to make solid eye contact with her, explained, "Whatever this thing is... I believe it's targeting the little boy."

Harmony's face turned from a look of curiosity to concern. By the nature of their work as well as having four kids of their own, experience warned them that anytime a child was involved, it was all hands-on deck and no time to waste for the duo.

Now, unfortunately, running directly over there was not a feasible plan. He knew you must separate emotion from a case. Although he wanted to rush over at that very second, it was not best for a successful outcome. He knew from experience that in this work sometimes slow and steady wins the race.

There were several things that Chris had to investigate before they could attempt to begin a physical investigation of the grounds. Not to mention that "work" in this field is much different than police or paramedic work. Again, they were stepping from the physical realm into the spiritual. In this world, firearm tactics, self-defense or even a degree will not help you.

When you enter the spiritual realm, you are entering their arena. Your weapon is faith in the one who is above the Devil himself...God. It was here, preparation was most critical. You cannot rely on the flesh when the flesh has no power over the demonic. This was always a humbling experience for the husband-and-wife team as they would have to have utter dependence on God more than their knowledge or skills. They would begin a few consecutive days of prayer and fasting in preparation.

Chris believed that when it comes to the spiritual world, it is not the chaos everyone believed. He would not be dealing with a myriad of spirits running around aimlessly with no purpose. In fact, it was much simpler than that but in the same way, much much worse. It would be a demon, a fallen angel with extreme intelligence.

He knew there are only a few players in this game. God and His Kingdom, the Devil with his minions and human beings of the flesh. Out of the three, only one is in Divine control.

A great misconception by those unfamiliar with the word of God is that the Devil is on an even playing field with Jesus. That could not be further from the truth. The truth is, that everything ever created, including Satan, the Devil, and the rest of the Demonic hierarchy, are subject to God in every move that they make.

He made a point to memorize scripture. *Colossians 1:16 of the New Testament was one of his favorites, "For by Him all things were created, in heaven*

and on earth, visible and invisible, whether thrones or dominions or rulers or authorities—all things were created through Him and for Him."

This Scripture made it very clear to him, that Jesus, God made flesh, created "all" things, whether in the physical realm or the spiritual realm and they were made for Him. As the creator, He was in control.

He also reflected on another example in the Book of Job of the Old Testament. In this book, God's most blameless follower came under attack from Satan. It was all for good reason in the end but the point to take away is that Satan needed permission every time to perform any activity on Job. And not just that, he was told by God, how far he can go in the activity. This is a very important fact to remember for anyone experiencing demonic attacks. God is still in control of your situation.

Chris was very knowledgeable on Theology, the study of God, as well as Demonology. Demonology being the study of Demons and the occult. In order to help those suffering, it was important to learn their tactics, maneuvers, and tricks they use to enter people's lives and educate them.

Chris found great use for the comparisons made between understanding the Devil's tactics and a famous 6th century BC book called, "The Art of War." This book, written by Sun Tzu, who is still listed today as one of the greatest military commanders in history, explained a very important point to understand that Chris brought into every case. When entering any battle...know your enemy. Chris had a lot to say about how this was an important concept to living a joyful Christian life but left out of many Churches. He firmly believed that understanding your enemy was half

CONNECTICUT - THE BEGINNING

the battle and needed for a continued victorious Christian life.

With no time to waste, Chris headed back into the office to begin the investigation. As he sat down, a quote was seen on the wall behind him in large black letters which stood out from the gray walls. The quote read, **"If you know the enemy and know yourself, you need not fear the result of a hundred battles. If you know yourself but not the enemy, for every victory gained you will also suffer a defeat. If you know neither the enemy nor yourself, you will succumb in every battle." (Sun Tzu, The Art of War)**

He opened the files and began to explore this odd-looking symbol which was the common theme to what was happening at this Connecticut residence. Chris opened his rustic looking book. It looked like something out of a castle that a wizard would use. A priceless gem of a book he obtained from a witch in one of his earlier undercover Ops. A witch that he ended up preaching the Gospel to.

In Chris's mind, he always believed that everyone needs to hear the Gospel at least once. It didn't matter who you were or what you did. This proved to be a good move on his part. The witch although not willing to change her beliefs at the time, had such great respect for Chris and his faith in Jesus, gave him the book to protect himself in the future.

As he turned the worn pages of the book, he passed through pages of witch's circles, spells, witch's tools, until he came across a chart of similar looking symbols associated with demons. Each was different in directions but similar in cause. Each of the black lines looked to have purpose being created specifically unique to each demon assigned to it. As Chris intently went down the chart looking to match this symbol captured in the attic, there it was!

As he traced the lines matching them up perfectly, his attention was drawn downward as he came across the name associated with this sigil.

"Marbas," Chris spoke the word under his breath.

Now he had a name to go by. This was a good start. He knew that specific demons were conjured up by people for specific purposes according to the demons' gifts. As he pulled out his other books from his little library regarding ancient demons, he began to talk aloud through his thoughts.

"Ok Marbas, who are you and what do you want with this kid?"

This part of the investigation is what Chris loved most. To be able to bring to light what is hidden and use the skills God has given him to bring out a greater good. This made him feel alive again. He recalled many years back, how he gave up any aspiration to advance in the NYPD but left the streets for ministry purposes. A decision that had haunted him for many years as a mistake until this new calling in spiritual crime fighting was dropped upon him.

Chris began the background into this specific demon throughout history. Marbas, first mentioned in the "Lesser Key of Solomon," was said to have a high ranking as a leader in Hell, with many legions of demons under him. From what he uncovered, Marbas was one of the first demons listed that presented with an intimidating stature and power to his seekers.

CONNECTICUT - THE BEGINNING

He was described as having the head of a lion and the body of a man. He will appear as a great lion but at the request of the master, take on human shape. In his notes to the side, Chris took a moment as if in deep thought and jotted down, "Is Marbas looking to take on human shape himself?"

Chris knew with the demonic, things were not always as they seemed. Their game was deceit. To deceive the naive into believing that the demon is subject to the conjurer, when just the opposite takes place in the end. The conjurer becomes the slave of the demon and ultimately its victim. Every demon had a dual nature. One nature to entice the person and the second to make the person its victim.

The gifting of this demon included healing of disease and the ability to give hidden knowledge. A power to give one an advantage over another. The conjurer will offer gifts to Marbas and in return, he will grant them a request.

He began to continuously jot down notes.

"Look for gifts left at the crime scene in the attic."

As Chris kept reading, he began to shake his head. The book stated in smaller print, "However…"

"Here we go," Chris thought to himself.

"Just like with medication, there is always a however," he mumbled with his head down reading.

CONNECTICUT - THE BEGINNING

"He can bring about disease and illness as well as cure it. Marbas can also control the actions of individuals against their will as well as set them free. Proceed with caution."

Another thing Chris knew is that you would always end up worse at the end than at the beginning when you play around with this type of activity. He had seen it time and time again in cases and he was expecting nothing different this time.

Chris looked for the angle of the demon and the invitation from the victim. The invitation would be the key to the case. At first, it seemed easy enough. A Satanic witch, a conjuring spell, a victim. But as he continued to go deeper into this puzzling case, he couldn't help but think that there was something else he was missing. Now introduced into our world, was this entity looking to do more than harass this family or was this the beginning for him?

But beginning of what? he thought. Chris once again moved his pen to the side column of his notes. He wrote in kind of quick chicken scratch, "Is Marbas looking for another invitation for something bigger?"

Chris stopped what he was doing. "Invitation," he said to himself. "Let's see what we can find on the prior owner."

Now that he had some background on the activity occurring in the home, it was time to find out why this started and who was the cause. He began to do a search on all of social media with the name given to him by Glenda. As the profiles were filing into his intake box, he knew this may be a long process since the name was not as unique as he would have liked.

As that continued, Chris began to look up information on the property. He went to real estate pages hoping the listing was still up on their page to get a look at the home before it was purchased by Glenda. As the page popped on the screen, Chris gave a pump of his fist into the air as a positive sign of confirmation. The listing was still there, and he wasted no time exploring each photo of the home. Hoping to find hidden clues that the average person would not even notice, he continued picture by picture.

Speaking under his breath, "Come on, give me something," as he kept scrolling with the mouse.

As he went from one real estate site to the next, hoping for a break, Chris found something very interesting on one page. A photo of the front of the house but something in the midst of the landscape is what grabbed Chris's attention immediately. Beautifully sculpted bushes surrounded by expensive cut stone were seen throughout the front yard and would draw in any potential buyers.

Directly in the middle of the landscape was a massive statue with a lion's face on it. Chris stopped what he was doing. He quickly opened the file containing the sigil in the attic on his left monitor. His attention swiftly switched to the monitor to the right! He opened the file depicting the image of Marbas, the demon's sigil.

"Lion? Maybe this is a coincidence." he thought. He knew it was not unheard of for some people to have animal statues in their yards.

CONNECTICUT - THE BEGINNING

At the very moment, Chris heard a bell notifying him that his search engine had completed the social media profile search for the owner. As he scrolled through a list containing many of the same names, what he saw next astonished him.

"You got to be kidding me."

As he just stared at the profile picture for this woman, it was if Chris was contemplating many different thoughts at the same time. Most, if not all the profile pictures that he viewed had a photo of a woman or maybe she had her family or children, But not this one. When Chris saw this profile picture, he knew right away that this was going to be a case like never before.

This profile picture was a picture of a lion. He slowly clicked on the picture with anticipation, not knowing what he would find next. Looking for a solid confirmation that this was the woman, he slowly searched the page.

Chris knew that in this uncertain world of spiritual warfare, real evidence is what is needed no matter how much you believe it. Yes, there was good evidence here that Marbas was at the center of the activity, but Chris wasn't satisfied. He needed to know this was the woman and what she was doing.

She posted very little about her personal life as he would have expected. The people that would post about their occult activities usually were nothing to be concerned with. He thought they were looking for attention or just a bunch of morons playing around where they shouldn't. The real danger was from those who practiced in secret. You would never see them coming. As Chris saw it, if this woman was the real thing, then we just caught a break.

As he looked at her check-ins and visits to her favorite spots, there it was in black and white. Stamford, Connecticut was used for many of her locations.

He took a sigh as he knew coincidence was no longer an option. Chris swiveled his chair as he turned away from the workstation and stared into the darkness of the room. He pondered questions in his head as he knew this was going to be a game of chess.

Chris and Harmony were about to take on one of the most powerful and intelligent demons known to mankind but not only that. He now believed that this was about to get a lot more complicated. They may indeed be walking into a battle that not only took place in the spiritual realm but in our realm as well. A human may be hunting them too. He needed to know more about this woman and if she was actually a threat.

There was only one thing to do next in his mind. Head out to Glenda's location and investigate.

CONNECTICUT - THE BEGINNING

CHAPTER FOUR

THE SKY BECAME DARK

2009, One year later, Chris and Harmony were madly in love. Life never seemed better for the two and they wasted no time moving in together. Harmony picked up her life from her Harlem apartment. Chris lived alone in a basement apartment out in Long Island. They had both felt so alone for so long wherever they were, but the feeling they felt when they were together was different and had taken that loneliness away.

Harmony had two young children, Jake and Samantha, ages eight and five, that she was raising on her own. Working around the clock some days, keeping the kids with sitters, and then coming home to be a mom, like so many in her position, was just physically and emotionally draining. It was taking a toll on her. To have Chris in her life now with a new direction and hope was an exciting time for her.

Chris was divorced and had two girls of his own, Sarah, eight, and Beckie, six. Chris, being a New York City Cop, made it very difficult to have any consistent time to see his kids, which left a hole in his heart. Losing his daughters as a full-time dad to divorce combined with the loss of his mother only weeks after, was more than Chris could bear. Harmony and her kids gave him a second chance to be present as a father in his own home and to be part of a family again.

THE SKY BECAME DARK

They decided to move to Long Beach, NY, where Chris's children lived. This would complete the perfect situation in their eyes. They would not only begin their new life together as a family but now Chris would have a life with his own children as well. The six of them would start over together.

But as we've seen time and time again in life, trials will test any relationship and will expose the flaws that are hidden in each of us. Chris and Harmony were no exception to this rule. After a short time, raising children together, commuting to the city on opposite schedules, trying to support two families on a city salary was already hitting the couple hard. Chris not only had to contribute to this household but had child support and other obligations for his girls. Tension was building.

The perfect relationship was facing some early tests, but this was never the real issue for Chris and Harmony. What the stressful job, the lack of money, raising children as stepparents and the time apart did was expose something much greater which would be the catalyst to what would be upon them in the months to come. If you asked them today, neither of them will tell you that what happened to each of them can be explained other than a miracle of God. To this day they still cannot explain the events according to the natural world. Unfortunately for the two, they were going to have to go through Hell once again to get there.

As I said earlier, there was a deeper issue that had to be dealt with. You had two individuals coming together attempting to be a family. They were two emotionally wounded creatures believing they would find peace being in the company of each other without first healing their own pain that each had carried for so long on their own. Chris and Harmony had been living separate lives, depending, and trusting only in themselves for a long time. This would be a recipe for disaster in any relationship, theirs being no exception.

As the relationship moved forward these issues began to go from internal pain to a physical manifestation through hurtful words and rage. They didn't know how to communicate or share feelings as people attempting to understand each other the way it was in the beginning. Shortly after that it became a survival of the fittest.

You may see the light of hope when you first meet that person of fate, but unless you both had made peace with your former lives, history shows, you're destined to repeat the process. This was usually the case in the past with Chris and Harmony, and it was happening once again before their very eyes. The yelling, the mistrust and tension were now affecting the children, who began to witness the self-destruction of the couple. This became a daily occurrence in their lives now. The next event proved to be the tipping point.

Chris was working the midnight shift and Harmony was still working day tours. It was around 9 pm in the quiet Long Beach town. It was a beautiful summer night in July. If you listened quietly, you could hear the peace of the waves crashing in the ocean just down the street. But inside their home was anything but peace. It was a ticking time bomb that was about to explode.

Chris sat in his recliner as he was watching the ball game with a nice cup of coffee before he headed out to the city for his shift. Harmony had just finished getting Jake and Sam ready for bed.

Harmony walked in the room and said anxiously, "Chris, I need more money. I have nothing to pay for the train on Monday for work and I owe the sitter. I am already a week behind."

Chris responded, "I don't have a dime. I barely have enough for gas and to pay the toll into work." As he continued to watch the game, his insides were beginning to stir with anger as he knew something was about to start.

Harmony replied frustrated, "So take the train, you get it for free! Help me out a little."

Chris, now getting upset, stood up and responded, "Help you out a little! Really? You're right, I haven't done anything for you and your children!"

He continued his rant as this was the set off point, he was waiting to unleash the built-up rage, "Yeah! I'll leave an extra two hours early and worry about some BS happening in front of me that I need to deal with before I start my shift!"

It was always a possibility for a police officer using mass transit, especially during the night, to witness some sort of crime that they would have to handle on their way to work. Chris felt there was enough to deal with on duty in the high crime area of Harlem, that he should at least be allowed to some sort of alone time in his vehicle heading into the chaos.

But that's not what really upset him. It was that this is another person that doesn't give a damn about him. He saw this as a personal attack.

Harmony didn't see it that way at all. She was seeing things from her point of view. The way she saw it was that she needed to get to work and be sure her kids were looked after between the shifts. She had responsibilities as well.

As the lack of proper communication continued, she yelled back, "Listen, we live in an expensive area, work more! I need to take care of my kids too."

Chris responds, "Your kids! Is that where this is going? Yeah, of course all you want is the damn paycheck, right? You know what? Why don't you work more? I'm done!"

As she turned away, Harmony could be heard under her breath, "I should have never moved in."

Full of rage now Chris with his porcelain coffee cup in hand, screamed, "Maybe, tonight will be the night I just don't make it back home alive and you'll get your wish!"

He reared back and threw a strike into the center of the wall with the cup. As it shattered into a thousand pieces, the kids began screaming in terror from their room as they were already awake from the yelling.

Harmony screamed, "Get out of our lives!" and went to tend to the kids.

Chris walked out and slammed the door with such fury it almost ripped the hinges off.

Harmony walked into the kids' room that was shared by them. Tears could be seen slowly rolling down her eyes as she tightly hugged both the children, consoling herself as much as them.

Chris walked the busy Beech Street in the West End which was a few blocks from the home. He noticed the nightlife was beginning to pick up. This was a popular area

THE SKY BECAME DARK

in Long Beach for Saturday bar nights. Tonight was no different as young adults began to fill the sidewalks in lines to get into their favorite pubs. Chris decided that tonight was going to be one of those nights for him as he called out of work. Not much of a drinker at all, he sat at the bar and decided to try drowning his sorrows like so many before him.

Chris sat there staring into space, nursing his drinks all night trying to find some peace during the continual destruction of his life. Even at the bar, Chris needed to try to remain in control. He would drink to relax but not enough to get out of hand. He wouldn't give it up too easily as was evident in his relationships. But tonight, he knew he exercised anything but control.

As he was walking around the town, he decided to go sit by the beach and watch the sunrise. This is something he has usually only seen from the windshield of a police car for many years. It was always the sign of hope for the midnight cops that the treacherous midnight shift would soon be over. What he witnessed this morning from the beach was something different.

Chris looked on in awe as the sun began to rise, outlining the few remaining clouds. As the dawn broke, he started to break down and cry for the first time since the night's incident. As he sat there pondering what had happened, he knew it was time to swallow his pride and go work things out with Harmony. He truly loved her and the children and now he needed her to know that he was going to do anything he could to make this work.

Chris jumped to his feet and with the new refreshing outlook that a beautiful sunrise brings to a new day, he headed back to the house with the same optimism. He stopped off to pick up the kids' favorite Sunday donuts and a nice cup of coffee to treat Harmony in bed. He was thinking he would also go pick up Sarah and Beckie and have a fun Sunday morning. It was going to be a day they all needed.

As Chris walked up the stairs to the porch, he could see his old neighbor, Mrs. Larsen, staring at him strangely. The homes on these blocks are basically lined up on top of each other, so Chris had a feeling that what happened last night was broadcast more than he hoped. As he reached to open the screen door, he could see that the heavy wooden door was wide open. As he stepped into the home, he abruptly dropped the bag of donuts and the coffee, spilling all over the carpet floor.

He continued into the front room, slowly moving his head left to right. Clothes and miscellaneous items could be seen thrown around the empty room. He gazed at the walls covered only with nails where pictures used to hang. As he continued to the kitchen in a state of shock, drawers were opened, kitchen utensils were all over the floor as if someone was sifting through the drawers in a hurry.

He walked back to the kids' room and dropped his head. He quickly noticed their favorite toys were gone. Even the pictures they made at school that brought their room to life as they covered the walls, were all gone.

Harmony had left him during the night. It was over.
Chris sat down on Jake's bed, grabbing onto a Hulk figure he remembered buying him for his birthday. The house was empty. The only things that remained were Chris's belongings once again. He was devastated.

THE SKY BECAME DARK

During the night, after Chris left the home, Harmony knew she wanted out and needed to remove her kids from here. As much as she loved Chris, hardened by life, she would do it alone once again. She was no stranger to these situations either. Heartbroken as well and in tears, she called her partner Lisa for a place to stay.

Like most partners in the world of first responders, Lisa came right over with a friend who owned a truck. In the Fire Department, as well as Police, there is a special bond between partners that exists. You put your life in your partner's hands, and they do the same to you. It is you and your partner against the world when you step into an ambulance or police car. That's who you are depending on for your life. One concept Chris and Harmony could never perceive in their own relationship and now it ended painfully for everyone involved.

As the two vehicles visibly stood out, doubled parked on this narrow one-way street, Harmony and her friends could be seen by the neighbors loading bags of clothes into the vehicles. One of the neighbors, John, an older man in his late sixties walked over to inquire.

"Harmony? Is everything alright?" he asked concerned.

Harmony still angry and looking to get her side out first replied, "Chris is crazy, and I can't be here anymore. I'm moving out now."

John, saddened by the news, responded, "I'm sorry to hear that. You guys looked so happy together. I can't believe it."

John spent time with Chris. He knew the responsibilities he took on with two families, not to mention a police officer. He had a lot of respect for both Chris and Harmony, as they worked dangerous jobs while juggling four kids. From the outside they looked as if they had it all together.

Harmony just stared at John with saddened eyes for a moment and walked back into the house. She didn't want this, and she also knew her part to blame for this as well. She didn't have time to reflect. It was easier for her to ignore her own issues at this point than to figure them out. She had too many responsibilities to worry about than fixing herself right now. She needed to continue forward and move on to the next place for the sake of her children. This was a pattern for Harmony going back to her teenage years. In her eyes she was helping them by quickly moving out but didn't even make the time to assess it.

Starting a relationship on passion and emotion was doomed from the start. The two lovers, who worked in an adrenaline-based job, with similar types of people, lived out their relationship the same way. Unfortunately, they brought their children into this boiling pot of emotion as it continued to heat up, thinking no one would get burned. That was hardly the case for all. It seems that there are always innocent victims who get caught up in the crossfire caused by the recklessness of others and unfortunately for these two families, this was no different.

Chris could not bear to stay in the empty home another moment. This was a scene that he experienced one too many times. He decided to head to his childhood home to stay with his father. Another relationship that did not end well after the passing of his mother six years ago.

The relationship between Chris and his father had always been a rocky one with blowups between the two. It ended with Chris and his father refusing to speak to each other much anymore after the death of his mother. Alone in the world and now without his children, Chris had to figure out a plan. He was broke. Trying to live on a New York City cop salary while paying child support, he couldn't afford much. He decided that he had to try to save money. He was too proud to ask for help, but he needed to find a decent place to have Sarah and Beckie for weekends.

Since Chris was still working midnight tours, he devised a plan. For the time being the girls would stay with their mother full time. He would finish his shift, drive out to Long Beach and park in one of the lots along the beach. He would sleep in the back of his SUV during the morning, wake up and go see the kids at his ex-wife's house in the afternoon. He was still trying his best to make life as routine for the kids as possible but for an adult it was anything but routine. He would then drive in to the precinct early and grab 3 or 4 hours of sleep in the bunk rooms before the shift and that's just what he did for the next several months until winter.

Chris attributed the love and purpose those two little ladies gave him for making it through that time. There were many times, aside from them, he saw no point in anything anymore. His daughters became the sole purpose for him to succeed and to survive.

His sister, Nicole, became the sole family member that he could depend on. He would stay over at her home with her family whenever he needed. She was always there with a helping hand or a shoulder to cry on.

Chris had never had the emotional relationship with his father that he had with his mom. It was always said in the family, that in looks and personality, "You're all your mother." Chris loved that. His mom was a sweetheart and a beautiful woman. Not a bad person to be compared to, he thought. She was something he missed dearly in his life when she passed away from pancreatic cancer at the early age of 55.

His father was known as an obnoxious tough guy. A real ballbuster with the forearms like Popeye which made him even more intimidating. He would fly off the handle at times for no reason and you could easily see he was not happy with his life as well. He had never once in his life told Chris that he loved him. Chris was no sensitive person on the outside by any means, maybe because of his upbringing, but it was something he always remembered about his father. Something he knew he would never let happen with his own children. They would hear it daily even at the end of every phone call. That is exactly what he has done even until today.

As Chris pulled into the driveway, he dreaded the conversation to come with his dad. It was early Sunday morning, his father would most likely still be sitting at the kitchen table drinking his coffee. This was what he did most mornings. As Chris walked into the house, his father turned around with surprise but not what Chris would have thought. He was happy to see him.

"Hey, look who's here!" he yelled with excitement as he stood to meet his son.

Chris just stood there a broken man. He grabbed his father and hugged him tightly as he began to break down into tears.

Crying and with each word he began to apologize, "I blew it, I'm sorry, I'm sorry if I embarrassed you."

"What happened?" his father asked as he tried to speak between the broken words.

"She left me." he cried. "Harmony left me all alone too. I'm all alone again."

His father knew of Harmony from conversation but never met her.

His father has seen this with his son many times through the years. As he broke the hug without any emotion, he walked back over to the table. He picked up his coffee, staring blindly at the TV as not even conscious of what was on the screen.

Without turning around he spoke out loud, "You can stay in your old room."

Chris, wiping the tears from his face, spoke softly with embarrassment, "Thank you."

As he turned around to head upstairs, he felt like garbage. A black sheep who was the butt of the jokes in his family. As far as he thought, they're probably right.

Chris slowly put his backpack containing a change of clothes on his old bed. The room was filled with baseball and football trophies from Junior High and High School. They were set in boxes by the door. He was surprised they weren't in the attic where he left them.

Chris was an accomplished athlete. He won the Most Valuable Player awards, one after the other, every year he played baseball. In 1989, his high school team won the New York State Championship. This was an amazing year. He won the Tournament MVP and days after, a full scholarship to play ball for Adelphi University.

A few years later he would be seen playing in the College World Series attempting to showcase his skills

THE SKY BECAME DARK

with all the others looking towards the Major League draft. But this was not the happy story that the events of his life pointed to.

    As Chris picked up a picture of himself in a little league uniform, he chuckled under his breath. As he continued going through the box, looking at picture after picture of his younger self, the memories of his past began to flood his thoughts. A recollection that was one of similar events throughout his life.

    In this picture, he was 13 and played shortstop for a prominent travel baseball team. As if he was thrown back in time through a color studded worm hole, Chris flashed back to one game in particular. One game, one event in time that he sought to forget his entire life. Now it was as if his past was colliding with his present and there was no running from it this morning.

    It was the last inning, and the game was tied. As a ball was hit out of his reach at shortstop, instead of diving for the ball which he knew he couldn't possibly grab, he decided to head to the cut off position to catch the relay from the outfielder. A decision he believed to be the smarter move to hold the runner to one base.

    As the inning ended, his team would come to the plate one last time in hopes of tying the game. Before Chris could make it to the dugout, his father took him off to the side in an area near the woods. He screamed at him, "If you are not going to try, then get the hell off the field." He continued ranting for what seemed like a lifetime to Chris, as he knew the others were watching through the open holes of the bushes.

    Chris was shaken up. A misunderstanding of why he didn't dive but it didn't matter. As he headed back to the dugout, he could see other parents and teammates pretending not to know what just happened. He was very embarrassed.

As he stepped to the plate with swollen eyes, he glanced back at his father. As he awaited the pitch, now with more pressure than usual for a last inning at bat, the pitch was on the way. Base hit! The game was tied. Fans could be heard screaming around the complex. His father jumping up and down as if the last 15 minutes never happened. The game was called on account of darkness and scheduled to be finished the following day.

Chris, staring at the picture in his room, was still in the same thought. Directly after the same game, he was sitting on the front steps of the house with his mother and father eating ice cream. His father is retelling the story to his mom and saying how proud he is of his son. "He really showed me something." he spoke proudly.

Chris kept looking down and eating, still sad from the events that took place. Thinking to himself, "I should have made you proud anyway."

His mother had no idea what happened earlier, and he never told her. But Chris learned one thing that day, no matter how good he was, he wasn't playing for himself anymore. It was something he had to do to make his father proud of him. He was now equating playing good baseball with capturing the love from his father.

The next day it all exploded right in front of him. As they continued the game, Chris was excited and ready to play. Unfortunately, Chris made two costly errors in the extra inning that cost the team the win. As he was heading home in the car with his father, the car came to a halt unexpectedly around the corner in the school lot.

THE SKY BECAME DARK

He turned and grabbed Chris violently, screaming at the top of his lungs about his terrible play in the game. He gripped Chris's shirt with such force, the collar tore open. Chris, feeling bad enough, yanked away from him and fled the car. He ran across the street to the apartment complex where his close friends lived.

They played phone tag and in moments, the group came together and huddled around Chris. They were a tight crew made up of boys and girls and were all best friends. They all grew up together since kindergarten. He was the athlete of the gang as they would come and cheer him on many times at his games.

As they were circling around him, Chris, still in his uniform, was telling them what had just happened. Just then, one of the girls spotted his father's car driving slowly down the block. He was looking for Chris. Suddenly, the car stopped, and a soft voice was heard from the car. "Chris, can I talk to you please?" his father asked.

The boys and girls stepped in front of Chris with dirty looks. Chris tapped them aside and walked towards the car as the boys and girls looked on. As they drove off, His father began apologizing as Chris looked straight ahead.
"Chris, I'm sorry, it's just that I want the best for you. You are better than I ever was at this game, and I want you to make it," he explained.

Chris's father was drafted out of high school by the Kansas City A's. He was a top high school prospect and an even bigger one in the A's Minor League system. Only a few years later, his hot temper that Chris was so accustomed to ended his professional baseball career. He would quit because he was not called up to the Major

Leagues on his own timeline. He packed up his stuff and came back home where he was not well received by his parents.

Disgusted at his decision, his father put him to work with him in construction. His dream ended abruptly, and he never emotionally recovered. He once said that he couldn't watch a Major League game for several years after returning home.

As Chris looked around the old bedroom, he came across another picture. There, he was a young man, both arms in a cast and bandaged up. Chris let out a slow exhale. This was just another memory describing one tragic event after another in his life. For one thing, Chris thought to himself that this was not what he needed today.

He was 21 years old at the time and still in the hunt for a professional baseball career. This, like his father before, was his identity. He missed getting picked up in the draft and was waiting on a tryout with the Texas Rangers. In the meantime, his father brought him to work construction with him. There definitely seemed to be a pattern with the DeFlorios. Chris was in the best shape of his life as he awaited the tryout. One blessing in disguise among the tragedy to come as he would soon find out.

As he and another worker were moving a 200-pound steel plate covering a hole in the street, Chris slipped and fell in the 20-foot hole. Before he could fall to the bottom, the heavy steel plate fell onto both forearms, suspending him in midair. As the men rushed over and pulled him out, he sat up against the curb and looked down as his body was in shock. He stared at his disfigured arms under his long sleeve shirt in disbelief.

THE SKY BECAME DARK

Chris remembered lying in the hospital bed as they rushed him into the emergency room. As his father rushed in from the other work site, Chris felt a moment of relief. With an IV of morphine hanging above him as he was in extreme pain and disillusioned by the medication, he cried out to his father for support. With tears in his eyes he asked, "What about baseball? Can I still play?"

His father in obvious emotional distress began to yell, "Baseball? It's over! It's all over!"

With that, a switch flipped inside of Chris as he tried to sit up, flailing his broken arms. He began to scream back with as much strength as he could muster. "Get out of here! I want you out of here!"

He directed his words to the nurses, "Get him out of here! I don't want him near me!"

Now the hospital room was full of staff from all the commotion. As the nurses were trying to calm Chris down from doing more damage to his arm, they were removing his father to the waiting room.

Chris had a surgical procedure done which involved metal plating inserted into both arms to help the fractured bones heal correctly. He was told that this metal would not have any negative complications and should not be removed over his lifetime. Chris found just the opposite was occurring, as shocks and pain became a daily experience with his new mechanical arms. His baseball career was over.

Chris was wheeled out of the hospital days later after surgery. He looked up at the sky for the first time since the accident. He thought to himself, "The sky has never looked so dark."

He lost his purpose. He lost his identity. Anything that was special about him, in his mind, was gone in an instant. He felt like a nobody with no direction. The 21-year-old, sitting in his wheelchair out front, waiting for the car to come around just stared at the sky.

He asked himself under his breath, "Have I just become my father?"

Chris, now back in the reality of his old bedroom, back in the present. He was feeling the pain once again. He sat back on the bed, looking down at his scarred forearms and uttered the words... "I have become my father."

Chris had reached rock bottom once again. He knew he had lost everything he gained on that fateful day. Was he just trying to fill the empty void as a paramedic and a cop all these years. How did he get here? Chris for the first time was digging deeper than ever searching for his soul. He stood up, walked over to the mirror hanging on the back of the door. He looked straight ahead and said in a heartbroken voice, "Who am I God?"

Chris was about to find out that his question was heard, and an answer was on the way.

CHAPTER FIVE

CONNECTICUT
The Cop and the Caregiver

Chris prepared the equipment he would need to investigate the grounds at this potentially demon-infested home. He took out two large black cases that were made of rigid plastic shells. This was to protect the expensive equipment.

He opened the first black case, which consisted of many different styled cameras tucked away safely in a soft but firm foam. The foam was cut out to perfection for the outline to each camera to ensure that the equipment would stand up to the test of any banging or accidental drop. He carefully inspected each camera individually as he proceeded to replace each battery with a full charge before heading over to the residence.

With his arsenal of cameras, including two body cameras as worn in the NYPD, he was ready to capture any activity for further review. This was an important part of investigating what he called spiritual crimes such as this. Most of the time, spirit energy was captured on photo or video footage. He found it was very uncommon to see it with the naked eye, so having cameras set up in strategic locations would be necessary.

CONNECTICUT – THE COP AND THE CAREGIVER

The GoPro cameras, camcorder, and full spectrum cameras to catch footage using minimal flash distortion filled the suitcase. He even used an ultraviolet (U.V.) light to inspect rooms in the dark with the hopes of exposing hidden evidence. Something he learned years ago from a detective at the NYPD Crime Scene Unit.

As Chris inspected his U.V. light, he remembered a case where he and his wife worked a couple of years back in Ohio. A family of five were having severe demonic activity in their home. So bad, they needed to leave the residence in the middle of the night and flee to a hotel. When they returned the next morning to quickly pack some clothes, they heard a noise. As the wife looked over her shoulder, the printer turned on and began to print. A page came down the printer with the words, "GO AWAY" in one continuous column, all the way down the page. The family fled the house and quickly called Chris.

When the home was inspected using the U.V. light, they were amazed at what was found. In large letters were the words, GO AWAY, covering most of the wall. This was a big clue to what was happening in the family home. The case was solved, and the family has since returned under the peace of God.

That is a big reason Chris decided to combine equipment and knowledge working together as one. Not every complaint is a demon. Furthermore, not every complaint is on the level. Cases can take twists and turns so you must be ready to leave your preconceived notions at the door and pursue the truth, no matter how painful or mind boggling it may be. So, a good investigator will use every tool that is available to him to seek this out.

In another case, Chris found himself in a power struggle with a Catholic Exorcist as they had a disagreement over what was happening in a home. It came down to solving the puzzle of what was causing the activity in a home in Westchester. The residence was plagued by the death of their animals, severe destruction to property and strange activity like water appearing on the ceiling. Chris and Harmony were not convinced that the house was under any spiritual attack.

By the end of the case, it was shown by Chris's police techniques, evidence, and the couple's medical training, that a teenager was causing all the commotion. Mental illness was the primary cause, and the devil was not involved. There was much more to the discovery but that's a conversation for another time.

As he opened the second plastic case, equipment used for detecting invisible spirits was tucked away in the foam. Electromagnetic field readers or EMF devices were used to capture disruptions that may be caused by a spirit in this field. Chris used these devices with caution. He knew there could be many different causes for energy spikes that could be rationally explained but many times he found them useful in coordination with other evidence he compiled on a case.

He then ran through his precious books one after the other that he would need just in case a blessing was required quickly. He was not planning to engage in a blessing on this day but there are no formal rules when you enter this work. The Devil never plays by man's rules. The only comfort Chris knew going into any case is that the Devil had to play by God's rules. That was enough for him to enter this line of work.

As he packed prayer books he used in the past, he made sure to pack his special book given to him with knowledge of these hidden occult secrets. This was especially important because there would be times when Chris would be at a loss as to what was occurring in the home and the information in this book was helpful on scene. He realized early on in this field of work the most important information you need will never be available in books for the public.

But what was most precious to him were his two Bibles. His English translation, that he used over a 15-year career in ministry to the Lord, ranging from feeding homeless, evangelism, and missions work overseas. As he turned the pages, encouraging scriptural notes and memories could be seen over the entirety of the book. He regarded this as the book containing his true identity, which was revealed only in Christ.

The second book was a Bible as well, but written in the New Testament language, Koine Greek. Chris learned this translation many years earlier wanting to pull out the true meaning that the apostles were expressing at the time. The way he saw it and probably in line with his personality, he did not trust anyone else translating their interpretation of the most important writings in history. This would prove helpful when he entered this "work."

He had another theory. He knew the Catholic Priests would use Latin when confronting the demonic because it was an early language in the faith. They had found that it would be an effective tool breaking down a demon. The way Chris saw it, why not go back to the original language of the times when Christ walked the earth? The time when we read about him casting out demons. He found this useful in other cases when speaking commands in a demonically infested home using the exact language.

CONNECTICUT – THE COP AND THE CAREGIVER

As he finished packing the last bag, Chris along with Harmony, headed out to the car to begin what would be known later by the two as the **"Lion Demon of Connecticut."**

During the ride there they used the time to prepare as well. Each one finding a way to relax before they reached the unknown. Harmony would zone out watching shows on her phone pacing herself for the busy day. Chris spent most of the ride going over the game plan over and over in his mind. This was the common practice for the two of them, case after case.

Before reaching a location, they would pull over to a secure location for prayer. Prayer was most important, and everything depended on it. They knew that everything they learned over the years would mean nothing if God did not show up.

As they were approaching close to the location of the home, the road swiftly turned from a wide two-way street to a winding narrow road. They were now moving uphill, with the thick trees of the woods lining the road on either side. They found themselves being pushed off to the side of the road more than once, as oncoming cars would fill the entire road. Combining the downpour of rain and dark, cloudy, sky, Chris found it difficult to negotiate the sharp, winding, turns as visibility became limited by the wooded areas. Chris looked towards his wife and said, "Would you have expected anything else?"

She replied laughing, "This is ridiculous."

It really was something comical to the couple who by now knew how to process this type of situation. Chris understood what he was dealing with from the interview and background check alone. In his train of thought, this was a spiritual battle now entering the physical realm. Anything would be possible from this point on in. A thought that would be strangely accurate as he would soon find out.

The rain let up as they pulled up to the house, it was anything but what you would expect from the car ride through the eerie wooded area. They pulled off the main road, driving through two 4-foot-tall posts made of beautiful stone on each side of the entrance. Chris perceived this to be the driveway which led to the home. It was a private road which then opened into three separate driveways. Chris was impressed. "Would you look at this." He spoke with amazement as he looked up at the homes to his right.

The houses were lined up on a small hill overlooking the land far off in the distance. Glenda's home was smack in the middle as it towered over the other two. At first look, you would believe this area to be the most peaceful place on earth.

Harmony gasped at the view but commented, "It's really something to think about. This is a classic example of looks being deceiving. Glenda probably thought she was moving into her dream home and now it's becoming a nightmare."

Chris responded in agreement, "Isn't that just like something the devil would try to do."

As Chris turned off the ignition, he looked over at Harmony and let out a slow audible exhale, "Think how jealous your friends would be right now if they knew what you were doing."

CONNECTICUT – THE COP AND THE CAREGIVER

As she was about to open the car door, Harmony looked back with a grin and responded with the same sarcasm, "True, I'll have to recommend this as a fun day trip for them"

Chris and Harmony activated their body cameras as they were greeted at the door by Glenda, her little nephew, and her sister, Bo. The videos did not do the women justice as they were both very attractive women. Glenda stood 5'1, blonde hair and fit and maybe 50 years old. Bo was a little taller with the same hair color and look. They were both Zumba instructors for the community which would explain it.

Both women were also very well spoken, and their personalities were very welcoming. Chris and Harmony felt right at home which would make the interviewing and investigation process that much smoother.

Her four-year-old nephew was just the cutest little boy. He wore a matching shirt and pants with a Disney character on them.

He had a speech impediment. He had a little trouble expressing his thoughts through words as Chris remembered Glenda explaining that he was special needs. Chris carefully but indiscreetly observed him looking for any signs related to the complaint given by his aunt.

Chris and Harmony greeted little Tommy. Tommy was very shy and bashful around the couple, as he continued to grip Glenda's hand. He would giggle, then withdraw to his aunt as he was checking out these two strangers in his home. Chris thought to himself and smiled, "What a happy little boy."

CONNECTICUT – THE COP AND THE CAREGIVER

Just the thought of an evil entity, let alone anyone who could attempt to hurt or deceive this little boy, angered Chris greatly.

He reached down in his bag and pulled out a little toy they had bought for him. He handed it to Harmony who crouched down to the child's eye level and handed it to little Tommy in surprise fashion.

Glenda shouted, "Wow, look at this Tommy, from your favorite show!"

Chris and his wife unknowingly brought a toy from his favorite show. This certainly broke the ice with Tommy. They had on-the-job training in these situations, since many times children would have to be interviewed in police situations or treated on an ambulance run. When working on a case such as this they both had their roles.

Chris was all about investigating and solving the case. It was said by good friend Stephen Doucette, who later accompanied the couple on a few cases, "It was like a switch flipped inside Chris when he pulled up to a location. You could see it in his eyes. All jokes ended, words became few, but his alertness and discernment jumped to a new level."

He felt responsible for his people and safety was always priority number one, especially when it came to his wife. Eyes had to always be on her. He was all business.

Harmony lived up to her work title. She was the caregiver. She was always drawn right to the families, maybe because of her heart for caring for people, but it was always evident at a case. She would put them at ease as they spoke about everyday life. She was genuinely interested to hear about jobs, family and even pets, which was always a favorite subject of everyone. She had a way of putting victims at ease, having them feel that they were in good hands, and it would all be ok.

Together, Chris and Harmony, with years of experience entering strange homes to aid others at the worst times in their lives became second nature. The moment they entered together they were in full control of working the room according to their giftings. It was easy to see that their worldly jobs were by no means an accident but just another example of the detailed preparation of God for their new vocation that He called them to.

As they all began to walk through the home, Glenda began to speak about the certain locations that activity was occurring. Chris planned on having a sit-down interview on camera but since Glenda was in full narration, he motioned over to Harmony to start recording. As Glenda showed Chris around, Harmony filmed the interview on the fly.

Glenda brought up the morning's activity immediately. She said, "Something must have known you guys were coming today."

Harmony curiously asked, "What do you mean?"

Glenda went on to explain, "Well, when I was outside this morning, I noticed the two garage doors were up. It's weird enough that it was open but to open both required separate actions. That wouldn't happen."

Chris went through the event slowly attempting to find a logical reason for it, but Glenda was quick to defend her position. She said, "I make sure the house is completely locked up at night before bed and there is no way that Tommy can open them even if he wanted to."

What she said next left Chris and Harmony scratching their heads. Glenda commented as Chris was about to ask another question, "Not to mention the home security alarm should've gone off and it didn't."

The couple looked at each other with concern as Glenda led them to the kitchen. As they walked into the kitchen, the first thing they noticed about the room was the size. The ceiling was high with a skylight, there was a huge island in the middle of the room across from the sink and stove. The area was spotless and in perfect order.

Glenda walked over to the countertop which held the block of knives. She explained, "When I came in from the garage I walked directly to the kitchen." She pointed to a specific knife in the block. She went on to say, "This knife right here, was sticking halfway out of the block. That has never happened before."

Chris looked closer at the knife in the block. He moved it in and out trying to gauge how tight the knife sat in the block. He then looked around and confirmed how neatly put together she kept her kitchen. At first, he was surprised that she would even realize she could pick out one knife sticking out among many. After considering how well she kept the kitchen, Chris concluded that it was absolutely possible.

As Glenda was elaborating on other activities over the past weeks, Harmony listened as she filmed. Chris would move around the room as if he were staring at something. More than one time as Glenda spoke, his attention was drawn to the stairwell.

Chris politely excused themselves from the view of the family. Harmony was looking intently at her husband as she looked to him for the direction he was thinking of in the case. She knew just by the way he excused them that he had something important on his mind. Chris said, "Listen, this is the real deal. You need to be on point today because we are not alone. The activity this morning plus the vibe I'm getting, like in the Pennsylvania case, is setting me off."

Harmony looked at Chris and said with caution, "Really? That's good enough for me."

They both recalled a time in Pennsylvania when Chris had the same feeling during an interview. That turned out to be one of the most demon infested houses they have dealt with to date. Things got so bad in this case that when the couple was performing the blessing in the basement, surprisingly a spirit manifested before their eyes. He was going to be ready this time.

As they walked back into the room, Chris spoke up. "Ok, let's get started. Why don't we start in the area where the activity was greatest?"

Glenda walked them over to the entrance of the attic on the second floor. It was not what he was expecting. The only access was inside a separate room, the size of a closet. The entrance was directly overhead and could only be accessed by bringing in a ladder. Glenda looked up with fear and said, "That's where it all started."

She said, "When you go up the ladder, you need to slide that wooden cover over to the side."

Chris asked his wife to hand him one of the GoPro cameras and a bottle of holy water as he placed his foot on the first step of the ladder. Chris began to perspire as he attempted to contain his fear. He was not excited about popping his head through an opening in the floor.

He slid the cover over to the right as it banged around. That was not as smooth as he would have hoped. Attempting to keep himself at ease, he looked down at Harmony holding the bottom of the ladder and said, "I guess the element of surprise is out of the question."

As he balanced himself on the ladder, with one hand, he gripped the floor just inside the opening. Using his other hand, he began to blindly douse the inside of the attic with holy water through the opening. If something was up there waiting for him, he was not going to make it pleasant.

As Chris moved upward through the opening, he couldn't shake the feeling that he was being set up. The high ground is the advantage, and he didn't have it. He moved up through the hole and entered the attic.

Chris looked around before letting Harmony proceed. Scene safety was drilled into the couple from first responding work as of first importance entering any scene. Chris saw a light bulb with a chain on the ceiling. He pulled the chain on the light for some visibility. As he looked deeper into the attic, the darkness lined the back walls where light was not available.

He pulled out his police issued flashlight clipped to his belt and flashed the bright light along the insulation lining the open walls in the distance. "All clear, come on up," he yelled to Harmony.

Chris walked the area with Harmony and Bo looking for evidence confirming suspicions he had found from his home investigation beforehand. The sigils from the videos were all painted over.

CONNECTICUT – THE COP AND THE CAREGIVER

Bo told them that during the week her and her other sister came into the attic and painted positive looking colors over the symbols. Her sister was a Christian and painted bright colors which read, "God is love" in many areas of the attic.

As Chris looked to the wall where he was first introduced to the sigil to Marbas, it was covered in bright blue and yellow paint. As he looked closer, he began to stare at the wall. He could see that the demonic sigil was coming through the other paint. It was an eerie sight. Chris began to tune out the women speaking as he inspected the wall.

Harmony came across something very interesting on the unfinished ceiling. As she looked closer, she was amazed at what she found. Bo, seeing Harmony's interest walked over to look as well. Harmony turned around and called for her husband. "Chris, look at this. Is this what I think it is?" She spoke with anticipation.

Chris took their place at the site. He couldn't believe his eyes, a bloody handprint! In fact, there were many handprints in a circular design. He looked over at Harmony and said with praise, "Nice catch honey."

Chris had always been the one in the spotlight working in these cases, but he knew very well that his wife had good skills. He knew how to let her know at every opportunity. As it would turn out, he would never work one without her again after the events that were about to take place in this home.

As they now looked around the ceiling for more clues, they found another bloody handprint followed by yet another until a perfect circle was overhead. Suddenly, Chris stopped what he was doing. He had a look as if he was on the verge of solving a puzzle or making a great find.

Without letting on to the two women, He turned to the picture of the Marbas sigil on the wall. Then without hesitation he looked at the paint covered sigil on the wall directly in front of him. Next, he turned to the picture describing a salt circle on the floor that he remembered seeing. He remembered making a mental note at home that it was across from the sigil on the wall. Chris looked down. He was now standing in the faded outline of where the salt circle once stood.

He knew what to expect in the next moment. He looked straight up at the ceiling. He shook his head up and down. He said with confirmation under his breath, "Now we are getting somewhere."

Harmony looked at Chris with confusion.

He let Bo know that he and Harmony would be up in the attic a little longer taking some video and had her go back to her sister to check on them.

Chris would never let on to families of their findings in the active investigation of a case. There were many reasons for this. One was that until all the facts are in, the family is at times being investigated themselves. For all purposes, he had to know for sure that the family themselves were not the culprits for this. This could be a real possibility.

Another reason for the secrecy was to not put any more stress on the family than they needed right now. Glenda had enough to deal with little Tommy, an ancient demon running around and not to mention a possible

Satanic witch leaving a curse. Yeah, that was more than enough in his mind.

As Bo made her way down the ladder, Harmony walked up to Chris and said in a low voice, "What are you seeing that I'm not?"

Chris slowly walked Harmony over to where he was standing. Just as a teacher might demonstrate with a student, he stood next to her. Holding her arm and lifting it, he pointed her towards the sigil on the wall.

As he pointed, he said, "Circle number 1, around the sigil." He then drew her attention to the floor at her feet. He said, "Circle number two, the circle of salt."

Now he had her full attention. Chris directed her to look straight up. When she saw it, she spoke it out as in disbelief, "Circle of blood."

He repeated her comment with conviction as when a riddle is solved, "Circle number three, The circle of blood."

Harmony walked over to inspect all three areas with the interest that a seasoned investigator would have discovering a hidden crime scene.

"Are you kidding me? Right under our noses!" she exclaimed. Reciprocating the earlier comment to her, slapping him on the back, she said, "Now that my husband, is a good catch."

Chris laughed. He said, "Maybe so but we have a much bigger problem. I think we are looking at a blood curse... blood magic."

CONNECTICUT – THE COP AND THE CAREGIVER

Next, they all headed outside to investigate the yard where this woman was said to have been dropping objects into the creek. As they continued the interview walking along the narrow hillside area of the yard, Chris continued to document with his body camera as Harmony recorded with the camcorder.

The area was covered with a beautiful rock garden containing massive boulder looking rocks as well. The rocks were set in all different formations, as some looked like they had been there for many years from nature itself. As they approached the edge of the hill, there was a steep drop into a running brook that separated the neighbor's yards. Between the two yards was a heavily wooded area.

As Chris looked on, he thought, "This is good cover if someone wants some privacy to do something."

Glenda began to tell them that this was the area where they spotted her at night. She said, "The neighbor could see a fire going in this area late at night sometimes. They were making sure the wooded area wasn't burning."

When Chris heard this, he changed his focus to the different rock formations since there were many. He walked up and down the area until he came upon one in particular. "This one seems to have the popular theme of the day, a circle of rocks," he thought to himself.

A rock formation, in almost the same size circle as the circle of salt. The rocks looked like one half of each rock was buried into the dirt, to be sure the circle was secure.

As Harmony walked over to Chris, he whispered to her, "Perfect size for a person to perform a ritual, don't you think?"

She slowly shook her head up and down in agreement.

Things were beginning to really add up in this little amount of time. With each clue, denying the possibility that someone was performing rituals at this location for who knows how long was fading. The question that was flooding Chris's mind was if this was an actual curse or a result of the prior owner's lifestyle infesting the home? The answer would make a big difference with what they were dealing with and who.

After interviewing the family and investigating the location for most of the day, Chris and Harmony headed home. It was time to look over the footage captured throughout the day and develop the case. Chris felt they had plenty to look over. It was now time to connect the dots while attempting to mentally process what they had witnessed today.

CONNECTICUT – THE COP AND THE CAREGIVER

CHAPTER SIX

THE RETURN TO OZ

The pickup truck moved slowly down the narrow street, Harmony with arms around her sleeping children on either side, stared out the window from the backseat with an empty gaze. As they pulled up to Lisa's Brooklyn apartment, Harmony took a step outside the vehicle and looked up at the apartment. Then as if taking inventory of the area, slowly looked up and down the block as music could be heard from a parked car not too far away.

She looked at her kids with saddened eyes and back at the surrounding area. With slow tears running down her face, she softly said, "Back where we started kids."

As they finished unloading the truck, Harmony put the children to sleep in a room Lisa had prepared for them. Harmony walked out to the den where she would be sleeping on the couch. As Lisa brought out fresh sheets and blankets to her, Harmony stood up and embraced Lisa tightly.

"Thank you, Lisa. I can't thank you enough for being here." she whimpered.

Lisa, tossing the blankets to the side, held Harmony. She responded, "Your family is my family. You'll get through this like you always have."

Harmony sat down on the couch and said, "You wouldn't believe the road I traveled, and I guess I'm still on it. Maybe there is no destination for me."

Lisa said, "Why don't I make us some tea and we'll talk about it?"

They both smiled as Lisa turned to walk away. Harmony knew at least for tonight she could let her guard down. Her partner had her back. A term used lightly by so many, but tonight it meant everything to Harmony.

Lisa returned to the room a few minutes later. She handed Harmony a steaming cup of tea and sat back in the chair across from her.

As Harmony took a slow sip as to not burn herself, she said, "Wow, this tea has some kick."

Lisa smiled and said, "An old family recipe," as she gave her a wink.

Harmony smiling back halfhearted replied, "I think you're going to have to teach me how to make it."

Lisa, now turning the conversation in a more serious direction, said to her, "You know, we have been partners for three years and I really don't know your full story. How did you get to New York City all the way from Michigan?"

Harmony looked at her and said, "Well, I'll tell you, but I think you better add some more of that family recipe to both of our cups first."

THE RETURN TO OZ

As Harmony was preparing to recount her story from a little girl in a small Michigan home, she almost felt as if she was back in that place. A place she wasn't sure she was ready to re-visit.

She began, "My father was a traveling musician who would be away for around three months at a time. I was five at the time, and my mother was sick most of the days with diabetes. We were living on welfare because although my dad would send money back, unfortunately it wasn't enough."

She recalled the large, cubed shape "block of cheese" as she called it, along with welfare checks for food each month. This became normal for me growing up. This went on for years. I remember one night while doing my homework, the lights turned off because we couldn't pay. When I was old enough to speak on the phone, I would get screamed at by collectors looking for my mom. She would be out working part time jobs off the books, so we didn't lose welfare. I had to lie many times about her whereabouts. I remember being so scared."

Lisa, surprised by what she heard, had stopped drinking from her cup. She was now drawn emotionally to Harmony's story. Lisa interrupted gently and said, "Honey, I can't imagine. You were still a baby."

Harmony, with a little positivity, said, "Well, something did start to happen in a good way for me."

She explained, "I loved to sing so I joined the choir in the Catholic school I was attending. I guess I was good because the teacher had my mother take me to auditions around town. Before long, here I am, an eight-year-old girl, singing in community theatre. I'm in lead roles playing

Annie and also Dorothy from the Wizard of Oz. I felt like I found something to take my pain away plus I really did love theatre. But something else started to happen."

"From the stress of seeing my mother sick with diabetes, the growing up in poverty and becoming independent at such an early age, I became anxiety ridden. I began to overeat. It became so bad that towards the end of elementary school, I was nicknamed Whale. So, I decided to use singing as a way to make friends. They would still make fun of my weight, but the singing kept me in the group."

"I looked happy to their faces but inside I was empty and hurt by the words. Many nights I would sit in my room, as my mother lay sick in bed, and cry myself to sleep."

Lisa's eyes began to well up with tears, her lips began to shiver. This is not what she expected from her tough partner. She began to think to herself, "She's been carrying this all these years and never showed it."

Harmony continued, "Singing is what brought me to New York City, to Broadway."

"My mother passed away from her sickness when I was 17. I graduated with a full scholarship to a college in Chicago not for theatre but for opera singing. The school at the time said I didn't have the "figure" for theater. That pissed me off."

"What they didn't know is that when my mother died, I went into a deep depression and lost tons of weight. I was a hottie," she said chuckling and proudly.

THE RETURN TO OZ

Lisa, thankful for the moment of levity, jumped at it and began to smile as well.

Harmony explained that since her scholarship was for opera, she couldn't do theater. She said, "I decided to make some calls to a friend out in NYC who worked theater. He would set me up with a vocal coach and some auditions for off Broadway."

"I said screw this, packed my stuff, left school without notice and headed here."

Lisa, very curious asked, "So what happened? Why are you on an ambulance?" She half smiled.

Harmony answered with a shorter and less descriptive answer than the earlier parts of the story. "Well, life happened once again. I met someone while working tables in a restaurant, I got pregnant, married with kids, and divorced."

She said, "And the rest is history. Hello partner!"

Lisa, blown away by the story, said, "Come here you," as she gave her a hug. Both women just rocked slowly as they embraced for a moment and let out a kind of exhale. Lisa knew what she had just heard was devastating and Harmony knew she had just relived something she had left behind from a time long ago and a place, far... far... away.

With that, Lisa slowly pulled herself away and lovingly said to Harmony, "Tonight you're safe with me, love you partner, get some rest."

THE RETURN TO OZ

As Lisa left for her room for the night, Harmony turned off the lamp and tucked herself in on the couch. As the bright lights of the city creeped through the blinds, only her eyes could be seen, as the darkness covered the rest of her face. She knew she was going to do anything but rest tonight, the timeline of events she brought back from her painful past flooded her mind. The quiet room was not her friend as she filled the space with visions of the children making fun, her mother's funeral and starting life at 17 all alone in the world.

Now, on top of the past, she was filled with the present-day tragedies in her life. The destruction of her relationship with a man she did love deep down, but on top of everything else was too much to weather. Her heart was broken once again. Harmony cried herself to sleep that night as she did so many times before, like that little girl in Michigan.

Chris and Harmony both had their eyes opened that night, forced to confront the painful paths they had followed their entire lives. Tonight, something was stirring in both of them as each revisited old pain as they came face to face with their past. What they didn't realize at the time was that they were set on a collision course with One Greater, who would change both of their lives forever.

A week went by, and things got worse for the broken couple. Chris attempted to reconcile with Harmony through phone calls but with each call came a new explosion of blame towards the other. No matter the good intentions, when each was backed into the corner, pride would be the result. It was a logical conclusion for two people whose lives developed according to the ways of the world, pride in yourself is power.

Once or twice, Chris would make a pass by Harmony's fire station during work just for a chance to see her face. One midnight during the week, as he drove by, he could see her sitting on the back of the ambulance. She was with three or four coworkers, smoking a cigarette and laughing together as they must have finished a call.

Chris saw that she was doing well. He felt sad, seeing that she moved on so quickly. He began to experience a range of emotions as the sadness turned to jealousy and anger. As he headed back to the precinct, he thought to himself, "I'm done."

For Chris, it was time to turn on his defense mechanism. He had a moment of clarity, which he would later call his "open window" many times through the years, but for today, he slammed it shut once again. The hope he felt from that morning sunrise on the beach as a new beginning just days earlier, seemed a lifetime ago.

As Chris pulled off, Harmony put out her cigarette and walked away towards the station next door. The further she went away from the group, the more the distractions to the pain they afforded dissipated. She glanced down the road, hoping to get a glimpse of Chris's police car circling the precinct area on patrol. The eight-year-old little girl from Michigan was still alive and well inside of her and though she became a master of emotional cover up on the outside, the little girl inside was heartbroken once again and alone.

As the week went on, the two were back to dealing with life as individuals once again. Not only in their perceptions as they always have but now in separate residences. Each would head back to their own responsibilities during the day with family, but sleep time would be the devil's playground.

Unknowingly to the other, both were held captive to painful thoughts, mistakes, and constant missed opportunities for a good life every sleeping moment. Sleep time became a time they both would approach with trepidation as it was the one place neither of them could control and would have to deal with their issues. It's the one constant area in the cycle of life that your guard is down. The conscious wall of defense is no longer present to stop that 800-pound gorilla known as the subconscious, which runs wild during sleep.

It was Saturday afternoon and Chris was walking around the backyard of his father's home. He was on the phone speaking to anyone who would listen to his side of the story. The blame game was now back in full effect. He was speaking to a mutual friend, when in an instant, something happened. Something that started a chain of events that would begin to reshape Chris's little world.

He was speaking to Tina, a close friend of his who had come to know Harmony over the past year. Chris first met Tina, her husband, and two children while renting the basement of their home a year before he met Harmony. They were a nice Christian family and in no time, treated him as if he was part of the family. He would babysit the little girls, eat dinner with them and attend family events. Chris knew there was always something different about them, something special. They were not just friendly but seemed to have such a genuine, welcoming love for someone they just met that he couldn't understand.

He recalled how every Sunday morning he would hear the little footsteps of the little children running on the floor above as they were heading out to Church. He would cover his head with the pillow as he tried to sleep. He respected their faith, but Church did not fit into his way of thinking. He would tease Tina often. Raising his hands in the air, he would turn away and say, "Good luck with all that," quoting Seinfeld, his favorite show.

As Chris was now on the phone attempting to tell her how mistreated he was by Harmony, she abruptly cut him off. She said, "Harmony told me these terrible things you did."

She was referring to the screaming, throwing things, hurtful words and probably many other things he was guilty of.

Chris stopped and just listened. As she was talking something began to happen. As he listened, he felt as if her voice was different. He couldn't place his finger on it, but it just seemed different. The voice itself, with each tone was tearing through layers of pride and tearing open his conscience.

As she continued, Chris began to change inside. It was as if he was looking into a mirror, but he wasn't looking at his physical appearance. This mirror revealed something much different about Chris. He felt as a person does when they are standing before someone who is much better than they are, only in this instance, the standard he was matched against was perfect.

It was as though for the first time, all the excuses and all the blame vanished. Chris was seeing himself, metaphorically speaking, naked and unprotected. What he saw at this very moment was not something he was proud of. It was as though he was given some sort of gift to see how he treated people, how he sounded and how he made them feel. His insides began to stir. He couldn't explain it at the time, but it was as though he was seeing himself up against what he should be...what he "ought" to be.

Chris stopped Tina, as his voice broke, "I don't want this life anymore, that's not who I want to be," he told her.

The tears began to flow steadily down his face. He began to sob as he felt his heart letting down his shields. If Chris was on the phone with a different person, he may have received good advice too, but now with his guard down, Tina's next words shifted his attention even more.

She said, "Neither does God. He has plans for you."

"God?" He thought.

Chris was trying to find an answer to every problem using his own understanding but now he was being told that there is someone else in charge. Someone greater who was mindful of him.

Chris had heard little things like this before. He always had a sense about God growing up. He knew there was a God, but He just didn't fit into his plans. There was something different about what he heard this time though. He was having an experience. One he couldn't deny.

He began to tell Tina what was happening during the conversation. He started to feel this strange hope and relief, like the feeling you get when diving into a cool pool on a hot day. He didn't have to feel this way anymore but more than that, he didn't have to be this person. He wanted to dive into that pool.

Tina, full of excitement and knowing what was happening to him, said, "Why don't you and Harmony come to our Church tomorrow?"

She and her husband were seasoned Christians and knew that God was doing something special today. Tina read about these stories of people coming to the LORD in the Bible and even heard many of them from close Church friends, but seeing God move this way with her involved, was a blessing for her as well. Unknowingly to Chris, they would pray for him to come to faith many times during their relationship.

She knew that he needed to hear something and knew Church was where he needed to hear it tomorrow. He was going to hear from God himself. The seed was planted.

Tina said, "Why don't I give Harmony a call and see if she will meet you there?"

Chris responded, "I appreciate that, Tina. I would love to see her again, but I don't think she'll go for it. I think it's over."

"Let me see what I can do. Hold on to that positive feeling. Have faith," she said. Chris hung up the phone and sat on a large flat rock under the tree.

"Faith," he thought.

He dropped his head and brought his hands together. He was tired and emotionally drained. With only the small bit of strength that he could muster up; he breathed out a few words that could hardly be audible to human ears. But it was not human ears that he would have to be concerned about listening today.

"Please help me God," he asked in a submissive voice.

It was only a few words but powerful words that one only needs to ask in times like these. God was bringing Chris to a place where he could understand this. It is different for each person as everyone travels a different road. Today, Chris's GPS was rerouted in a totally different direction. The question was, was he going to trust it this time or stay on the same route he has taken his whole life?

Jake and Samantha, as though last night were a dream, sat there watching cartoons as Harmony cleaned up the lunch dishes. Lisa got called in to work to fill in for coverage, so the Brooklyn apartment was empty today. Harmony wanted to be sure not to impose, so she was sure to pick up after the kids.

She was thinking she should call her aunt out in Michigan. Harmony began to contemplate returning home to some family. She was not too happy about returning to the city life with the children. She would have to take a lot into account as she would also need to find work out there.

Was this what she wanted though? Harmony began to second guess her decision to leave Chris so hastily. Just as she did many years ago, running away from pain, she did it again in a moment. She still loved Chris but now she looked to run back to Michigan. A place where all this pain began.

THE RETURN TO OZ

Harmony took a moment to sit down. She was tired. The continual running of her mind took a toll on her physical body as well. Her eyes were heavy, her face was pale, and her wavy blonde hair thrown up in a scrunchie. As she sat back on the couch holding the phone in one hand, trying to figure out her life, she closed her eyes gently.

"Please help me," She whispered under her breath not to draw attention to the children.

Harmony, raised in Catholic school, was no stranger to basic prayers taught over the years, though they were nothing more than educational teaching in a school system to her. She never had "real" faith or an understanding of a "real" God.

When she was a teenager back in Michigan, one of her older cousins who was a Christian, came to her. She tried to speak to Harmony about God. Harmony, who had just lost her mother to Diabetes, had no interest hearing about a God who loved her so much that He would take her mother from her at such a young age. As her cousin wouldn't take the hint, Harmony made it clear by slowly blowing the smoke from her cigarette in her face, getting up and walking out of the room.

This morning, another apartment, another couch, and another direction was just too overwhelming for her. Though on the outside, she would hide it from the kids, inside was pure emptiness and hopelessness. She began to see that she was creating the same pattern for her kids as her own childhood. This was not the life she was going to have for them.

THE RETURN TO OZ

As she sat there on the couch, her cell phone rang. It was Tina. Not sure if she was in the mood to speak to her again, she let it go to voicemail. She just spoke to her a little earlier and didn't have anything new to say.

Not even listening to the voicemail that popped up, she decided to call her aunt. As the voice at the other end picked up, Harmony had a look of confusion on her face.

"Aunt Betty?" she asked.

"No, it's Tina," she replied.

Harmony said confused, "Tina? That's the strangest thing. I was dialing my aunt."

Harmony didn't realize that when she went to hit the button on the screen for her aunt, that Tina's missed call notification popped up at the same time. Without knowing it, she hit the button and called Tina back.

"Well, since I got you here. Let me ask you a quick question."

Harmony responded, "Sure, What's up?" Harmony was thinking maybe it was something for Tina.

Tina said, "I just talked to Chris..."

Harmony cut her off, "Tina, not now please."

Tina pleaded, "Just listen, I just had a very interesting conversation with him. He sounded very different."

"Different how?" she asked.

"He has a lot to tell you," Tina told her.

Tina continued, "You should talk with him, you'll see."

Harmony was intrigued at this point. Deep down, she always wanted their relationship to work. She was really looking for any sign of hope. Maybe she should hear him out.

Harmony said, "Maybe I will."

What was happening to Harmony was different than Chris. As Chris was beginning to have a major experience he could not explain, Harmony was not. She was interested in possibly reconciling her relationship with Chris. She wanted healing in her personal life, in her relationship, but was still not looking inward. She just wanted things to work out.

Tina knew that Harmony was taking baby steps and not ready for the same message Chris was. She listened to Harmony speak and decided to let Chris tell her about Church. She thought that it might sound different coming from him.

"Ok, great! I'll have him call you." Tina calmly but joyfully told her.

Later that day, after Chris finished pacing the yard and getting his thoughts together, he mustered up the courage to finally call Harmony. He was anticipating a cold reception.

She answered, "Hi" in a soft voice.

"Hi Harmony, how are you?" he asked.

She replied, "I'm ok, hanging in there, how are you?"

They both could feel a sense of longing for the other right away. Chris came right out with it, "I miss you."

Harmony feeling the emotion as well responded, "I miss you too."

Chris now felt a powerful urge to open up to her and tell her how he felt. Something he didn't understand how to do until today. "I want to apologize. I had no right to speak the way I did to you and treat you that way. I know I was wrong, and I don't want to be that person anymore. I would like another chance to show you."

As Chris continued, Harmony just sat there taking it in as Chris went on and on with this new outlook. But what was more shocking was that he was expressing his feelings for her with such clarity and emotion, something she had never heard before. He wasn't holding back, he left himself vulnerable and seemed willing to risk being hurt again. Chris said, "I was talking to Tina, and I think she had an interesting idea. She invited us to her Church tomorrow, you want to give it a try together?"

After hearing all of this, Harmony replied, "Church? Wow, I didn't see that coming."

Chris just listened to the silence for a moment, wondering if he passed from what sounded like a guy fighting for his girl, to gone off the deep end. He didn't care. He knew something just seemed right about it.

Finally, a voice at the other end of the phone, "Yes, let's go. I think it's a great idea."

Chris was overjoyed and relieved at the same time.

"Awesome, I'll find out the details and get back to you a little later."

This was nothing like the other phone calls during the week. She could hear the sincerity in his voice and at that moment, she needed to hear it. Before the call she sat there heartbroken but after she spoke with Chris, that was not the case. As she hung up the phone, she was overwhelmed by a peace she had not felt in a long time.

She sat back on the couch and said, "God, did you just answer my prayer?"

God was moving in their lives, just as He has always been. The only difference now was that their eyes were being opened to it. Their world was about to get a lot bigger.

THE RETURN TO OZ

CHAPTER SEVEN

CONNECTICUT
Marbas and the Child

There may be some people who would take a little time to relax and unwind after an investigation like this. In fact, it would probably be a very smart move, but that was not how Chris operated. In his mind, there was way too much happening to sit back and wait. How could he go back to regular life and pretend everything is fine in the world, when a family is under attack?

Chris would often leave Church after a Sunday service very uneasy. He found it hard to reconcile hearing an amazing message by a pastor to go out and make a difference in a hurting world, but in the same service get pumped for the football game in a couple of hours. To him, this was one of those moments. Should he turn on the TV for a fun movie and relax or seek a resolution for this family who is dreading going to sleep tonight?

Chris was removing the video cards from all the cameras and recording devices. Harmony, always her husband's biggest supporter, pushed open the door to the room with a nice Italian dinner they had picked up on the way home. As Chris began to upload file after file, she placed the sweet smelling, chicken and eggplant parmesan dinners and soft garlic bread at the folding table in the corner. This was their idea of a nice evening together.

It was now evening on Monday, the next day. Chris was out with Sarah and Beckie running some errands. He took the week off as his 50th birthday was a couple of weeks away. They were out picking up supplies for his party that the family was planning.

To the outside world, the DeFlorios were just your everyday family. Chris, would be seen out front in the summer after returning from work, talking with his retired neighbors. Talking about their kids and life but mostly whose grass was looking better. This was always a favorite topic. He never spoke about this part of his life and as far as most people knew, they were the average American family living next door.

Just then, Chris received a troubling text message from Glenda. He looked down to read the message, it read, "Tommy is making lion noises all around the house. He never did this before."

Chris's face turned pale, and his daughters noticed it.

"What's wrong dad?" asked Sarah.

He looked up, "Nothing honey," he replied.

Acting as if he didn't just receive a message from Glenda he was hoping would never come, he attempted to change the subject. "What color theme is Harmony putting together for the party?" he asked.

Beckie jumped in, "Nice try dad, was it about a case? I know it was, what happened?"

CONNECTICUT – MARBAS AND THE CHILD

Beckie was the one who was always in dad's business when it came to this ministry. Although he attempted to keep this part of his life secretive to the kids for the most part, she always had good instincts. Beckie was highly spiritual and understood the spiritual aspect of life very well. Chris always wondered in the back of his mind if she would be called into this type of work. A calling he absolutely did not want for her or any of his kids involved in but then again, he knew it would never be up to him. Unknowingly at this moment, it would be something he would have to make peace with in the years to come.

Chris replied to both with a little smile, "Not happening."

He told them, "It's ok I will get back to them later. It's fun night out" as he zig zagged the cart down the aisle jokingly.

Beckie grabbed her dad's arm with a seriousness he was not expecting and without even having any knowledge of this case, she said, "What if it's a family like ours? What if something bad is happening over there right now?"

Chris looked down at her as she finished speaking. He then looked towards Sarah, who gave a confirming look at what was just said.

Sarah said, "Go call them dad, we get it."

Chris's eyes began to slightly have a watery look to them as he heard the things being said by his own kids. He was overwhelmed with a mixture of pride in his daughters for their maturity and the encouragement to do what he had been called to do. This greatly encouraged Chris.

CONNECTICUT – MARBAS AND THE CHILD

One of his favorite movie scenes was from Rocky 2. Adrian, while in the hospital, gave Rocky the go ahead that he desperately needed to fight. Rocky smiled with excitement and relief as it was the push he needed to succeed. Chris felt he was having that moment with his daughters.

It was something he battled for years internally as he was away many times, focused on different types of ministries in service to God. He knew he was a blessed man as they all were very supportive in helping others. This was a push he needed knowing it was going to be a long case.

"Ok, thanks, I'll be right back," he said as he walked to a secluded part of the store. "Hey Glenda, what's going on?" he asked.

"I'm not sure," she replied in a worried voice.

"Tommy used to make these cute little cat sounds mimicking our cat. Today, he suddenly started making loud lion roars."

"Did you ask him why he was making these sounds?" he asked.

Glenda replied, "Yes, I did."

She continued, "I asked, is that the sound our cat makes? Tommy, shook his head no."

"I said, who is that? He said that weird name again, Meshaw or Shaw."

Chris cringed. He let out a deep breath as he looked up into the corner of the store ceiling, deciding how to answer this. He was well aware of what was going on now, but he had to be wise in his response. Telling an aunt that there is a demon pretending to be a lion and trying to possibly possess her nephew was probably not the way to go.

"That Meshaw name again," he replied playing it safe.

Wanting to buy some time, he said, "Let me go look at some things tonight and call you first thing tomorrow. But if anything else happens at all, please call me right away, no matter what time."

It was 5:00 a.m., Wednesday morning. Harmony was still lying in bed, half-awake as Chris was already up on his second cup of coffee.

"Ready for some coffee honey?" He asked.

She replied, "Yes, please."

This was their routine every morning. Harmony, constantly fatigued by Lupus had always had Chris on edge. She handled it like a champ, but he could see how tired she looked working almost seven days a week as a home health aide trying to help support the family. She seemed to have found a new calling caring for the elderly on Long Island. She quickly gained one of the best reputations in this field and has kept many relationships with families even today.

As Chris was making his way to the bedroom, coffee in hand, he made a jerky movement as if he almost fell. It happened right in front of the opening of the bedroom door, where Harmony had a perfect view lying on her side. She popped up her head, "Are you alright! What happened?" she asked almost laughing.

He replied, "I tripped. I tripped over Chevy."

Chevy was their 13-year-old little dog. As he got older, it was not unheard of for him to get in your path at times unknowingly. "Chevy is still sleeping. He's over here in his bed" she replied, pointing to the foot of their bed.

Chris's face turned to confusion.

I'm telling you, I just walked into something and tripped. "I thought I kicked him in the gut. It was that solid." He continued, "I almost fell on my can."

Just then they both stopped and looked at each other as if the same light bulb went off in their heads simultaneously. Chris knew he should have been looking for this sign and was annoyed he missed it.

After a Florida event a couple of years back, the DeFlorio household turned into what can only be described as a circus. Unexplainable activity became a common occurrence for members of the family.

The Roomba vacuum began to activate on its own during night. The hours would range from anywhere between 1 and 4 am. Chris, seeing that the times were inconsistent, ruled out any programming issues and began to document, looking for something to connect the times. After a week or two, the activity amped up.

Chris was working the 2019 New York City Marathon detail. At around 6:00 p.m. as the street sweepers were cleaning up the streets after the long day, he received

CONNECTICUT – MARBAS AND THE CHILD

a call from his wife in a panic. She told him that Samantha, who was taking a shower, saw a dark shadow walk by the other side of the curtain. She opened the curtain quickly and saw no one there. She closed it again, began to shower. Moments later she heard a very loud growl. She ran out of the room shaken up.

Harmony had an experience of her own. She was cleaning the living room. As she bent down under one of the tables, all the items on top of the table fell onto her head. In disbelief of what had just happened, she walked by the stairs overlooking the basement. She took a double take as she saw a shadow moving across the floor. Now one incident away from complete hysteria, she looked closer as she could see a man wearing a cloak with the hood up. He walked right down the middle of the basement floor and then vanished.

This activity became something they were accustomed to during a case. It became a signal to the couple that a case was extremely serious. But more than that, they knew they were on the enemy's radar now, as in the case at the Florida resort which started it all.

Up until today, the interesting factor was that Chris had pretty much never been in the line of fire like everyone else with this type of activity. It was as if those around him who were more susceptible to fear, or confusion were the targets. What concerned him now was that whatever this thing was, it had no issues about going after him.

He thought to himself, "This thing either wants to scare me off of this case like the one who tried in Florida, or its powerful enough to just physically take me out. How did I not see this coming?" he said, shaking his head.

He was always his biggest critic and expected himself to live up to perfection. A burden that he learned to mostly overcome from his childhood, but still stuck its ugly head out at times.

Harmony said, "Ok, so now we know what to expect at least."

Chris looked at her in agreement but withheld his true thoughts. Being that he was a lot more invested in the updates of the case and seeing it develop daily, he knew the activity in his own home may be worse than ever before.

Later that day, Chris received another call from Glenda. As he picked up the call, he could hear text message notifications going off at the same time on his phone.

"Hello, Hey Glen..." Chris attempted to say but was abruptly cut off by Glenda.

"Chris," she said with a bit more urgency than usual. "I just sent you two videos that you need to look at right away please."

Sensing panic, he tried to slow her down to get the story. "Nice and slow, let me know what happened in your own words before I take a look."

This was his way of also testing if what she was actually seeing was in line with the video. One of the first things he learned interviewing people as a cop or a medic, was never to ask lead in questions. Let the complainant tell you in their own words first before you offer any insight.

CONNECTICUT – MARBAS AND THE CHILD

After he wrote down her account, Chris told her he would look through the footage and call her right back. He opened the first video and began to explore. It was a video of Tommy. Chris looked without surprise as if he was expecting nothing else.

Little Tommy was playing in his bedroom. Chris could tell from the questions Glenda was asking Tommy, that Tommy must have just said something profound and was trying to get it on video this time.

As she filmed, Glenda asked Tommy, "What was the name in the attic?"

Chris sat there listening in anticipation for Tommy's response.

Tommy quickly answered as he continued playing, "He's Shaw."

Glenda without hesitation, "He's Shaw?"

Tommy responded again, but this time pointing up in a very quick motion and while turning towards the camera, "Shaw's up there."

Chris looked on as he ran his hand over his beard covered chin. But what he heard next was chilling.

As Tommy continued in his answer to his aunt, he tried his best to express his thoughts. With eyes slightly off to the side of the camera, he looked at Glenda. He quickly raised both hands and held them in a way as if someone was making attacking claws for hands.

He said, "He make sound like this...Roarrrrrrrrrr!"

Tommy emphasized the roar as a lion would when he is calling his dominance over a kingdom. It was just amazing how this was documented on camera in the child's own words and undeniable at this point.

The next video was even more troubling for Chris. Tommy was walking around near the door that leads to the attic. Glenda very wisely began to record him, just as I asked. In the video Tommy is seen opening the door and attempting to walk in.

Glenda, immediately asks, "What are you doing Tommy?"

Tommy responds, "Going inside."

Glenda asked, "Why do you want to go inside?"

Tommy looks at Glenda with a bashful smile, like a child who just got caught doing something he knows he shouldn't be. He begins to swing back and forth on the door and points to the attic in one quick motion.

"Inside," he simply says.

With the ladder still standing up, it looked as if his intention was to get up into that attic. This was progressing much faster than Chris had experienced before. He quickly called Glenda back to ask a few questions to rule out some things.

"Did Tommy ever look to get in that room before?" he asked.

Glenda responded, "Nope, he has never tried once or has ever had any interest in the attic area. In fact, I don't think he knew it was there."

Chris asked, "Do you think he could have seen us going up at the house and maybe became intrigued?"

Glenda replied, "I don't see how since I took him outside and sent Bo with you."

Chris shook his head in agreement. That ruled out any prior knowledge or curiosity from Tommy. This was rapidly passing from what's known as an infestation of a home to the possible possession of this child.

The demon was singling out the little boy. He had two things working against him. First, he was a child. Innocent and vulnerable to being deceived, as children are with devious strangers. Second, he was special needs. He had a disability that he was battling and difficulty communicating his thoughts. Combining both, he was an easier target for a demon who is looking for an invitation to manifest somehow. This thing was making it clearer by the day that he chose his target.

Chris made the decision after this new information came to light that he needed to bring in the Church to handle this. As he always said, his overall mission was to lead people back to the Church and more importantly to Christ. Since Glenda did not follow a specific denomination anymore, he had to think carefully how to proceed.

Though She had a background early on with the Baptist community, he pretty much knew off the bat that unfortunately the Evangelical Church was off the list. After many disappointing interactions with them when it came to requesting help for someone, he realized it was something most pastors were not willing or equipped to handle.

Remembering a case in the Bronx where he and his wife helped an older woman, Chris told her afterwards that she will need to follow up with her pastor and listen to his instructions. When Chris called to follow up the next week, she told him that her pastor said that his works are of the devil, and she hung up on him.

Chris continually found himself at the door of the Catholic Church. They seemed to have the high ground on the subject when it came to understanding these matters. But more than that, they truly believed that this activity was real, and had clergy in place to help people. They were going to be his choice in this matter as this was his only option once again.

Chris immediately looked up who to contact and reached out through the proper channels. After a couple of emails, he was set up for a phone call the next day with a priest involved in handling these types of requests. He took a moment to thank God for getting him through extremely fast, since it would usually take much longer.

Late morning the next day, Chris was on the phone with the clergy member who would decide where this case would go next. Chris introduced himself, sharing his background and faith. He then began to explain the story in detail and the chain of events from start to finish.

The priest was very impressed and taken by the story. Chris then sent over some of the pertinent footage captured as evidence. The priest was quickly on board with the same findings as Chris, this family is in trouble.

CONNECTICUT – MARBAS AND THE CHILD

He told Chris straight out, "This looks like the real thing, I can see you're the real deal, and I agree. We need to get involved quickly."

Chris was overjoyed. Now he believed those more qualified would see this through and this family would get the help they needed. As well, He was praying that Glenda, and her family would find Christ during this time. This was of course always most important to Chris and Harmony.

The priest told Chris that he would most likely get back to him next week and let him know how they are going to proceed.

In the meantime, since he was still on vacation, Chris decided to make another trip out to Glenda's home. Harmony was working, so he headed there alone. There were a few loose ends he wanted to tie up while he waited on the Church to respond back. One, was to look more carefully for any type of witch's tools in the attic and the ceremonial spot in the rock garden. The other was to interview Tommy directly. Something he knew would be a challenging situation.

As he arrived, Glenda told him that Tommy was still at school and would be arriving home in an hour or two. Chris was fine with it. This would at least give him some time to look around the sites. He pulled out his flashlight and made his way to the attic.

As he entered the attic, he could be heard saying in almost a comical but serious manner, "Ding, ding, round two."

He pulled the chain to the single bulb light. As the first time, it lit up the immediate area of the few wood floor planks that were nailed to the floor beams. The floor planks contained the salt circle and some sigils. He looked into the darkness of the attic where there was no flooring and no lights.

He thought to himself, "If I was looking to hide something, that's where I would do it."

Now that he was only responsible for his own well-being, he didn't think twice about heading into a more dangerous area.

The outside temperature was in the 90's and humid. Inside the attic, he felt it had to be over 100 degrees. As the sweat began to pour down his face, he turned his baseball cap backwards and proceeded towards the dark areas of the attic.

Carefully, he stepped on each narrow beam being sure to balance himself. In between each beam was pink insulation that was not welcoming for sweaty skin. The insulation was resting on nothing but sheet rock which made up the ceiling of the second floor. He knew that one slip off the beam and Glenda could have a new unwanted entrance to the attic.

As he made his way to the wall in the back of the attic, he couldn't help feeling that he was being watched. Call it nerves or plain old fear, but he had an uneasy feeling.

As he made his way around, using his NYPD issued flashlight for his direction and good old New Balance sneakers to get him there, he spotted something leaning on the wall. It didn't look as if anyone was too concerned with hiding it as it was in open view. It was a long rectangular piece of finished wood. The wood was spray painted over with the same color paint the sisters used over the Marbas Sigil.

Chris removed his hat for a moment, running his hand through his sweaty hair for relief as he pondered the find.

"Where the hell did I see this before?" he asked himself.

He took the board as he walked over to the square opening leading to the 2nd floor.

"Glenda," he shouted, "Do you remember painting over a long piece of wood like you guys did with the walls?"

Glenda yelled back, "Hold on, I'll give my sisters a call. They were the ones painting up here." After a few minutes, she yelled up, "Yes, that board had a large pentagram in the middle. She painted it and tossed it away from the area."

"That's it!" Chris recalled.

He quickly took out his phone and pulled up the early videos of the attic filmed by the sisters. As he scrolled through the moving video, he saw something and went back. There it was, the same board in the background, unpainted, just as Glenda had described it. He knew what this was used for. It was a Witches table that was used to hold her tools on while creating a spell.

Chris realized since with all that was going on their first visit, this board was not even in his thinking. He took the board and placed it down on a sheet Glenda threw up to him. From his pocket came a bottle of holy water. He began to bless the board, slowly wrapped it up and moved it to his car. He would later remove it to an unknown location.

As he stored the table away in the trunk, he removed a pick and shovel. A closer look on the home computer of the possible ritual site in the yard, he became fixated on this handle of some kind of tool sticking out of the ground. This handle had some green paint on it that he also spotted around certain areas of rock in the yard. He was curious to see if there was any relevance. He was going to dig it out.

As he began to wind up and slam the pick into the ground, he could see this was going to be difficult. The ground was extremely hard. He wasn't making much progress before he felt a crack. The handle broke in half and that was it, put it to bed. Luckily, he got deep enough where he was able to remove the object by pulling it out with his hands. It was a very long screwdriver which was planted deep in the middle of the circle of rocks. Not sure why this was here, he decided to play it safe. He blessed it in the same manner as the table and removed it to the trunk. Just as he closed the trunk, Tommy's bus pulled up in front of the house.

As he ran to his aunt's arms, happy to be home like any child would from school, he spotted Chris and after a slight hesitation of confusion to his daily routine, he went back to jumping around. The three of them entered the house, went into the kitchen, and sat around the table.

Glenda brought snacks and juice for Tommy. As he sat there expectantly, Chris could tell that he looked forward to this every day after school. Glenda then sat down at the table with blank paper and a bunch of crayons. Tommy eagerly reached for them and began to scribble as he ate his snacks.

Before Tommy returned from school, Chris and Glenda spoke out Chris's idea. He knew since Tommy had some difficulty explaining in detail what he was experiencing, maybe he could draw it. The plan was for Glenda to ask Tommy about it since she is the person he was most comfortable and open with.

"Tommy, would you draw a picture for Chris?" Glenda asked.

Kicking his feet over the floor beneath him as he sat in the chair and ate. Without looking up and still chewing, he stared shaking his head, bouncing it up and down to the swinging of his feet indicating yes.

As Tommy was scribbling, Glenda stopped him. "You know what? Could you draw Meshaw for Chris? He wanted to see what your friend looks like."

Tommy smiled and giggled playfully as he began to draw. Chris couldn't see much as he sat on the opposite end of the table. He looked on as he could see Tommy making wide, unsteady movements with his hands as the crayon seemed to move all over the page.

He didn't expect too much. After all it was a four-year-old little boy. As he drew, Chris was thinking back to a cute drawing Beckie made him around the same age when she first realized daddy was a police officer. She always wanted to be his partner. It was a drawing of her, then a plus sign, then daddy, both in police uniforms. It was followed by an equal sign showing a robber in jail. He smiled as he still had it on the wall at home.

Chris watched the subtle movements and facial expressions of Glenda as she watched the paper intently. It was his only window into what was coming into view. She gave a glance towards Chris, widening her eyes for a moment. He wasn't sure what to make of it. When Tommy had finished, Glenda took the page, wrote at the bottom right corner, "Meshaw" and the date. As their eyes met with blank stares and seemed to stay locked, she slid the paper over to Chris.

Chris leaned forward in the chair as he examined the drawing. He could make out a large, light brown circle taking up most of the page. Coming directly out of the circle in a darker brown color, were many individual straight lines. The lines covered an area from about the four-o clock to eight-o clock positions moving counterclockwise. The bottom of the circle looked like a bunch of squiggly lines making up some sort of beard on a face and was colored in the same dark brown. Inside the circle were two very large, unproportioned red circles with a long red half circle along the bottom.

Chris didn't have any reservations about what he was seeing. It was a lion's face. The large circle with brown lines coming out was the lion's mane. The thick portion of the mane was drawn around the chin. What was most terrifying about the drawing was the red eyes and what looked like a devious smile on the face.

He thought to himself, "Holy crap," (only he didn't say crap).

Chris quickly headed back home with the drawing. He knew he just made his case much stronger to the Church. As he headed back for the two-hour trip home, he dialed the office of the priest he had been communicating with. He was met with a voicemail that he would be out of the office until next week.

Chris yelled in the empty car, "You got to be kidding me!"

He then emailed him to get his attention. Chris knew that time was of the essence. This little boy had no qualms about the appearance of this demon in lion form. That told Chris one thing, that a worst-case scenario was in the making. Tommy showed no signs of fear from the spirit, in fact it was as if he befriended it. It wouldn't be long until he was grounded enough and claimed his right to stay.

As the week went by Chris waited impatiently for a return call from the Church and to show them the new developments. He knew this would expedite their involvement.

Finally, contact from the priest. He was hoping for a call but instead an email.

It read;

"I'm sorry for the delay in getting back to you. I have spoken with our Archdiocesan director of healing and deliverance Ministry, who directed me to the Diocese of ...., in which the home is located.

Here is what they suggest:

CONNECTICUT – MARBAS AND THE CHILD

Although your intentions are good, without the proper training and oversight of the Catholic Church, as well as acting outside of the sacramental life of the Church, your advised to stop. You are strongly encouraged to come back to the Church, for your own Spiritual good.

A member of the impacted family should contact the office of healing and deliverance, and they will work directly with the family.

Again, please be assured of my prayers.

Yours in Christ.

Chris was angered by the callousness of the response.

He said, "Yeah, so another words, you're not a member of our group. Obviously, you don't know what you're doing, so have them give us a call and we'll see.

The more he thought about it, the more he became furious. He knew this was just more political nonsense masked under religious language. He thought, it was interesting how the first priest he spoke to could sense he knew what he was doing and was ready to move but the higher up he went, it was denied.

Chris couldn't get past how the decision was made without even a conversation. Not a call, nothing. In his mind, he knew he couldn't trust where he would have to send this family who had grown close to him and his wife in this short time.

He thought to himself as he re-read the email, "You know what, I don't know anything about him either. This guy could have his own agenda."

Chris called Glenda to tell her what had transpired. Though he knew how he felt, he also knew that the right thing to do was to give Glenda the option.

He said, "Well the Catholic Church got back to me. It was not what we were thinking." Chris continued, "They told me to remove myself from helping, and for you to call personally, if you need their help."

"What?" she replied surprised and a little annoyed. "Why should you stop? You and Harmony were the only ones who would help."

Chris replied, "I guess I'm not in good standing with their organization and apparently, I'm not trained as a Catholic."

Glenda replied hastily, "No way, you guys are staying. We're not leaving you. Bo and I trust you two."

"We don't go to a specific Church for that matter, especially a Catholic Church and this is exactly why. This stuff. All these religious organizations have an agenda. There is always a catch to get some help."

Chris heard the disappointment mixed with anger in her voice. He told himself before the call that he was going to be led by whatever decision Glenda wanted. She now made it very clear.

He looked over at Harmony who was aware of what was going on in the conversation. She looked at him with very passioned filled eyes. Chris knew what that meant. His wife was a fighter and did not do well with B.S either. This was not the first time they had to deal with the bureaucracy of the Church and innocent families being left on their own.

Chris took his hand off from covering the phone and looked straight ahead as if he was going to speak. He knew if he decided to stay, that they were on their own and that things were just heating up. But they really didn't have a choice; a little boy was in imminent danger and that was all that mattered.

"We're not going anywhere." he said as he hung up the phone.

He looked at Harmony and quoted his favorite Biblical scripture in these moments, **"And the Lord sent them on ahead of him two by two."**

Chris walked towards a big black bag in the corner containing the blessing kit. He began more of a preliminary overview of the bag as he was still running the last moments of the phone call in his mind. He saw the burnt covered brass censor which looked worn from overuse from many cases. Then two large bluish containers filled with holy water, anointing oil and a large jar of blessed frankincense. These were just a few items he would bring with him back to the infested home. Chris zippered up the bag and prepared for the head-to-head battle with Marbas.

PHOTO SECTION

PHOTOS

Me (all smiles) in the NYPD Plain Clothes Unit. 2008 and Harmony FDNY EMS 2009.

(Left to right) Myself, Harmony, Sarah, Jake, Beckie, and Sam at the 32 Precinct kid's Christmas party 2008.

PHOTO SECTION

Harmony and I, Long Beach, 2010.

PHOTO SECTION

Rare picture of me playing ball during my years
at Adelphi University

PHOTO SECTION

Parade detail towards the end of my career and prank "wanted poster" by detectives after cops claimed to be assaulted by a spirit in the 32 Precinct bunkroom.

PHOTO SECTION

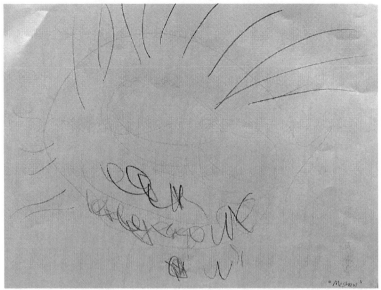

Little boy's drawing of spirit making contact with him, Connecticut case.

In a separate case, a little girl was experiencing demonic oppression. The above drawing is what she saw.

PHOTO SECTION

Sharing the Word of God at the school in Africa 2018.

PHOTO SECTION

Myself with the children in a remote village in Rwanda, 2018.

Bloody handprint we found in the attic during the Connecticut case.

PHOTO SECTION

Attic cover dislodged by entity, Connecticut case.

PHOTO SECTION

Harmony and I performing a house blessing, 2021

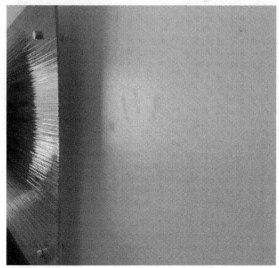
Mysterious handprint found in girls' room, Florida resort, 2019.

PHOTO SECTION

Photo capturing entity in girls' room, Florida resort, 2019

Marbas Sigil discovered in Connecticut attic (Photo by Roberta C.)

CHAPTER EIGHT

THE SKY NEVER LOOKED SO BLUE

July 12, 2009. It was a sunny morning in Valley Stream, Long Island as Chris and Harmony pulled up to the Church. They didn't know what to expect since both came from Catholic upbringings. As far as they have been told in the past, this was supposed to be different. It was a "Born Again" Church, not that they had any idea what that meant.

When Chris heard that word, he always thought of something from when he was about 10 or 11 years old. His mother brought him to some little Church service that was not like a Catholic service. The memory was always hazy but one thing he never forgot. He looked around the room and people were raising their hands with their eyes closed, At the time, he thought the people were crazy.

As they pulled up to the Church, they were surprised to see that it was not much different to what they were used to. The building was massive. It was made of red brick with stained glass windows just as a Catholic Church would look. There was a tremendous cross affixed to the building directly over the entrance. On the other end of the building was a high mounted steeple that you could see far in the distance.

The couple arrived, walked through the doors into the lobby and were eagerly greeted by people with programs in their hands. Chris and Harmony arrived very early, looking to sneak into the building undetected. They wanted to get in quietly and find a seat in a pew away from anyone but that was not going to happen.

It was as if a new face stood out right away. Hello, is this your first time here? Welcome, I'm so and so, nice to meet you were being thrown all around in the lobby towards them. They began conversing with these complete strangers who, to usually skeptical Chris, seemed very genuine.

They made their way into the sanctuary. The couple was caught off guard by what they saw. It was as if they walked into one very open auditorium. The two looked at each other with confusion as this was something they had never seen before. They scanned the room in an almost circular fashion, as if someone might be looking at a beautiful home in awe.

Harmony looked at Chris, she said, "I have a feeling we're not in Kansas anymore." A line she spoke many times throughout her life as a child actress.

The front of the room had a large platform which was filled with musical equipment. Drum sets, microphone stands with electric and acoustic guitars standing up next to amplifiers could be seen across the stage. It was as if they were getting ready for a concert.

As they walked down the aisle, there were no pews. There had to be a couple of hundred individual seats lined up in sections of rows around the auditorium. To the back of the room, was a huge balcony section that could hold probably 100 people alone. "That's insane" Chris said as he marveled at the sight. As they turned to look for seats, Chris pointed to the right side of the room, near the back end. "Let's sit over here so we can get a look at everything."

He was referring to having a clear view of who was coming up behind them as well as seeing what's happening in front. Police officers are trained to basically have their backs to a wall when in a room to see anything coming. This was well known among Chris's family.

He taught his girls at an early age to observe people and places when they were out. You could never be too concerned about the safety and protection of your kids as he saw it. Why would you withhold educating them to what could one day save their lives or the lives of others?

It became a game with the girls when they went to a diner or somewhere. They would race to be the first to point and say, "That's daddy's seat." to this day, they still know what seat to keep open for dad.

Service was beginning as the once empty sanctuary was filling with anticipated worshippers. The pastor walked out as the band followed to their assigned spots and picked up their instruments. Everyone knew to rise, except Chris and Harmony, who looked around and jumped to their feet a little embarrassed. They could not imagine what to expect.

"Let us worship the LORD!" he shouted in his microphone as the music began to play. The place came alive to a steady beat as if getting ready for something big. Then a beautiful voice of a woman with background singers filled the room. Chris looked down as he noticed

Harmony already moving to the beat. He tapped her and gave her a smirk as he looked at her dancing feet. She just kept on going, not minding what he thought.

Then the clapping began. The entire crowd began to clap to the beat of the music. Chris still didn't know what to make of this. Harmony already seemed to be letting go as she was seen clapping along and smiling with those around her.

"I don't recall this in my Church growing up," he thought thinking back to Catholic Mass as a kid.

The words to the songs were very moving. Speaking everything about Jesus and how He cares for us.

Chris and Harmony began to listen more intently to the lyrics. Harmony was feeling something she had not felt in a long while, peace. Her whole life was based around music and this different genre that she was being exposed to for the first time, began to break down her fortified walls.

As the guest preacher stepped up to speak, they were both anticipating what was coming. The 20-minute worship that you may think was a long time prepared them for what was to come next. They became focused on what was happening in this sanctuary and let go of all the worries that they first walked in with.

The preacher spoke in depth of how Jesus cares for you. "When you feel alone, you are never alone. God is there waiting for you. Your Father in Heaven loves you, come to Him." He said, "Jesus knows you're not perfect. He loves you because He is love, not because of anything you must do. His love is unconditional. Come to Him."

THE SKY NEVER LOOKED SO BLUE

He went on to say, "God will forgive you of anything you have ever done. Anything in your past is never too much for God to forgive. All you are to do is ask for forgiveness and come to Jesus."

Harmony's heart was overwhelmed with emotion as she sat there listening. At that moment, she felt as if it was only God and her in that large auditorium. She had so much guilt from the past that she never acknowledged. Personal things that she thought could never be forgiven. Hearing this was like hearing life for the first time.

The preacher went on to say, "HE will make you new," and displayed a scripture in big lettering on the movie type screen behind the platform. ***"The name of the LORD is a fortified tower; the righteous run to it and are safe." -Proverbs 18:10***

Harmony was tired of being alone, never finding a person and carrying a burden of guilt for what seemed a lifetime. When she saw this scripture come to the screen, she started to slowly tear and was ready.

The Preacher asked everyone to stand.

"If you're here today and you hear the voice of God calling, step out in faith and receive Him. Come up and kneel at the altar," he said in a loving voice.

Harmony, standing with eyes closed, not caring about the multitudes around or what they would think, was about to push past Chris. She was ready to run to God. Just then before she could open her eyes, she felt a warm touch on her hand.

Chris leaned over and whispered, "We have to go up."

Harmony was thrilled and surprised. Earlier in the service he was horsing around but now he wanted to go up front with hundreds watching.

What Harmony didn't realize was that as God was spending time with her during the service, He was also continuing the work He started on Chris yesterday. The message on forgiveness now made sense after being exposed to his true nature yesterday in that one little phone call. Today, he heard something he needed to hear his entire life.

When Chris heard the message that His love is unconditional and there's nothing you must do to be loved, he broke down. He never heard anything like that directed to him about a Father. Something was happening over the past two days he could not explain but one thing he knew, he didn't care. He wanted what was being offered to him for the first time in his life.

He grabbed Harmony's hand and the two made their way up front. They noticed others moving up to the altar as well, but it didn't matter. In their minds, God was there for them today and nothing was stopping them from coming to Him. They knelt as now the lead pastor of the Church took over and began to speak specifically to those who were up front.

He said, "God sees you this morning. He knows your pain. He sees your faith. Give your life to Him and you will leave this place a new person, with a new direction in life. Leave everything at the altar this morning."

THE SKY NEVER LOOKED SO BLUE

The pastor spoke with such love and such authority. They felt as if God was speaking through him. His words were cutting through their worldly defenses that protected each of them over a lifetime. They were up there with nothing left to hide. Christ was all they wanted.

As the pastor stood over everyone walking back and forth speaking this message, he noticed Chris and Harmony. They stood out from the rest. The two of them on their knees with eyes closed, were crying uncontrollably. He immediately walked over with the guest pastor and placed their hands upon their heads.

He began to speak over the Church, that it was ok to feel emotional and to let it go. Let God clean out everything in your lives today. People from the congregation left their seats and came up behind the couple. They placed reassuring hands on them as the entire Church knew something was happening to this couple this morning.

Chris spent a lifetime watching his back in a room but this morning he left everything out there up at that altar. He trusted and he believed that whoever came up behind him in that moment was sent by God. He was changing. "Praise God!" could be heard throughout different areas of the Church as the service seemed to turn towards Chris and Harmony.

As the crying continued, the pastors kept praying. After about ten minutes of continual cleansing, Chris and Harmony were lost in their own place and time with God. They opened their eyes to see themselves surrounded by a large group of people who honestly seemed to care for them.

They slowly stood to their feet as complete strangers hugged them and encouraged them. Chris and Harmony weren't sure what just happened but many of those in the Church certainly did.

They started to say, "You just got saved!"

At the time, the couple had no idea what that meant but it sure sounded ok with them. They spoke with the pastor on the side for a few minutes after the service. He was very interested in speaking further with them sometime to hear their story. He was genuinely interested.

As Chris and Harmony made their way out of the Church, with reddened eyes from what seemed a lifetime of tears, they hugged and shook hands with many in the lobby. Women were already exchanging numbers with Harmony, while men hearing Chris was a cop, wanted to meet up soon.

As they walked out the door holding hands, they smiled at each other. That was the one thing that was overlooked by each of them on this fateful day, their relationship. It was all about God. Their relationship took a back seat as the healing began in their own lives individually.

They stepped out of that Church, July 12, 2009, as new creatures in Christ, transformed by his sacrificial love and found a home that was eternal. Now it was time to begin the healing in their physical relationship as well and under the loving guidance of their Father in heaven. They would no longer go at this alone as He would transform this area of their lives too.

THE SKY NEVER LOOKED SO BLUE

Chris stopped and noticed something in the Sky above. His pause was noticeable to Harmony.

She looked at him and asked, "What's wrong honey?"

Chris still staring upward said with a peaceful smile, "The sky never looked so blue."

THE SKY NEVER LOOKED SO BLUE

CHAPTER NINE

SPIRITUAL WARFARE BEGINS

Weeks went by following the radical conversion of Chris and Harmony at the Sunday service. The couple moved back in together with the children. Things were much different now as they would watch Christian shows together and go to their new church as one big family.

They noticed odd things such as cursing disappeared from their lips as well as how they handled situations more calmly. Harmony quit smoking basically overnight which she couldn't even believe. God was cleaning them up and beginning to do a work in them.

Many events began to occur in their lives, events that would be called supernatural. They were highly trained over the years from their worldly jobs as first responders, but now new training had to begin for the "other world" they were being called to. New training in spiritual warfare.

When most people hear of spiritual warfare, they think of taking on the devil. Well, that's true, but there are two kinds of warfare. The first is individual spiritual warfare. This is where you learn how to live your new Christian spiritual life apart from the flesh and through the temptations of the devil. This is very important because if you cannot submit to the Lord here, you cannot even think

SPIRITUAL WARFARE BEGINS

about the second kind of spiritual warfare of battling the devil for others in our world.

Harmony, now working in Brooklyn as dispatch for the Fire Department, had the first experience in her new training. During one of her breaks, a coworker approached her as she sat outside to get some air on the Brooklyn Street.

She began to talk to Harmony about this change she had seen in her over the past weeks. How Harmony almost overnight handled the stressful calls coming in, that she stopped cursing and how she even gave up smoking cigarettes cold turkey. She was amazed and asked Harmony what happened.

The coworker said, "I want what you have."

Harmony replied, "It's all Jesus. You need to ask for forgiveness, turn away from the things you've done and give your life to Him."

The woman asked, "Would you pray for me?"

Harmony turned pale as she was struck with fear. She was only a Christian for a few weeks and did not feel she was ready for something like this. She saw the pain on the face of her coworker and knew she had to try.

Harmony replied smiling, "I'm really new at this but let's give it a try."

The two women held hands right there on the busy city street as Harmony began to pray as best as she knew how. After the prayer, they hugged, and the woman smiled as she wiped the tears from her face. Harmony gave a sigh of relief when it was over, feeling this was more stressful than the 9-1-1 call she just handled inside.

She learned something herself in that moment. It wasn't so much of how well you speak as much as it was letting yourself become uncomfortable and step out in faith. Something she would need to remember in the years to come.

Chris's return to work on the other hand was a bit more radical. Before the conversion as we will call it, let's just say he would not be called a Christian at the precinct. A mouth full of obscenities, obnoxious joker with a temper to go with it.

Not long before the big church event, Chris was having difficulties at work. He was placed on something called "force monitoring." This was not a list to be excited about. It meant a cop had too many complaints of using unnecessary force when conducting police activities.

In all fairness, most of the time they were unsubstantiated complaints that perpetrators would make purposely after an arrest, or a ticket to try to hurt the officer in some way. Either way it caused issues in his performance as he was given a stern warning to tone it down or be taken off the streets for a while. This was becoming a last straw with the job in his mind after it seemed the fight against the job itself was becoming harder than working the streets.

Back when he first started patrol at the precinct, he was ready to make a difference as most cops coming out of the academy felt. He soon partnered up with a fellow rookie, Rich. The two rookies together amid senior cops on a midnight tour did not go over very well in the beginning.

Always looking to be the first to respond to the action, they were soon on their radar and shut down.

The senior cops had good reason to feel this way. Two rookies with no real street experience could be a dangerous situation for all of them. They could either get someone hurt by doing something stupid or by when the senior cops would have to come to their aid in a hurry.

Chris and Rich did not disappoint. They were not only in the middle of the midnight action or maybe even causing it in their precinct but also in the neighboring 28 Precinct. They couldn't wait for the weekend to come because you could be sure in Harlem, sectors would be running all night from job to job. But as with most professions with rookies, it was expected that they would be running the errands no one else wanted for that shift. Chris and Rich seemed to be doing them more and more, which was becoming noticeably apparent and frustrating to them.

It was a Friday night in August, the streets are packed, Chris and Rich are working 32 David, The busiest sector in the precinct. Chris was already at the car when he looked back to see his partner talking it up outside the precinct. Rich would never miss an opportunity to tell a story as everyone waited around in front of the stationhouse for the 4x12 shift to come in. He could tell a story like no other. But the issue was that the food run was always the priority out the gate for the inside senior cops of the midnight tour. That was not something they were looking to do on a night like this.

Finally, as Rich is standing around, The old gray haired senior cop hands him a food order. It's 11:45pm, as these two rookie cops stand in line at Wendy's all the way uptown. The radio blows up with activity. Both of them begin to fume as they hear sector cars running all over the place and here they are looking like dopes in their uniforms ordering food which did not go unnoticed by the crowd.

They decide to put an end to this by eating half the food on the way back. It took two more errands, but the senior cops got the point and that mysteriously ended the food runs.

Another time, they were at the ER entrance at Harlem Hospital. Rich was inside checking on one of the midnight cops sitting on a perp. Chris was outside in the car talking with one of the medics he used to work with at that EMS station. As he looked to his right, he could see a guy take off his shirt and walk towards a woman in an aggressive manner. That's a telltale sign that something is about to go down. He lifted his arm, as Chris immediately threw the car into drive and raced over there.

In the meantime, the medic ran into the hospital and told Rich, "You better go help your partner."

As Chris pulled up to the scene and began to open his door, the shirtless man took off running down the sidewalk. Unknowingly to Chris, Rich was already on foot running up to the police car. As he just grabbed the door handle, Chris took off, almost dragging him down the road.

As he made a hard right turn at the corner, Chris didn't realize that he forgot his door was not fully closed and almost flew out the driver's side door. Rich, watching Chris hanging halfway out the door put a pursuit over the air. Now everyone is flying to the scene.

SPIRITUAL WARFARE BEGINS

Chris exited the car and chased him up three flights of stairs. As he tackled the guy in the hallway of the building, he could hear sirens getting closer and closer. Not thinking they were there for him, he walked the perp down the stairs. To his surprise, he saw close to 20 cops on the scene about to run into the building. It felt like a movie premiere with everyone watching him arrive, but after a minute, the action film turned into a comedy.

"What do you got?" asked the salty Sergeant working patrol for the night.

With most of the cops in listening distance, Chris replied with a blank look, "He ran?"

This didn't go over well as the Sergeant kindly explained to Chris what he did wrong. That part was a joke as you could imagine.

You run the risk of getting someone hurt rushing to a scene whenever you put over an emergency call for help, so it better be good. That was a lesson he never forgot as he thought about it over and over for weeks while sitting in the precinct answering phones.

After this new experience that Chris found with God, he started to see things differently. He still was motivated to help others but in different areas as well. He started to look and act different, so much that his old partner Rich, who he once pounded the Harlem streets with, would playfully call him a Jesus freak.

In 2009, as if God put it there, a lot of his focus changed to helping the hurting and homeless. He started doing this on his shifts while the activity slowed down and it caught the attention of fellow officers. He developed

SPIRITUAL WARFARE BEGINS

friendships with a lot of the people living in the streets in the precinct area during that time. Harmony would make food and Chris would go sit with them under the scaffolding. As he would sit with them sometimes two or three in the morning, he would give Bibles and food.

Chris started to experience something transforming in his heart as he began to see that it's not what's on the outside but the inside of a person that matters. Something he knew very well in his own life but was never able to understand in others until now. These weren't just people who didn't want to work or were just lazy but people who had their own stories. They were people who suffered and had great loss in their lives whether children or families.

Many times, he could not believe the stories that he was hearing and even learned many lessons from them as some of them were much older than he was. One of the blessings Chris realized from this type of ministry was that not only was he helping others but by helping them, he was receiving a blessing. Many of these people became friends of his.

So, Chris and Harmony decided to take it a step further and bought prepaid cellular phones for the ones they were caring for on his shifts. They believed it would be very good for those alone when they hit tough times that they could just give Chris a call and talk on the phone. It would give them instant access instead of hoping Chris was coming around again.

There was one man named James who lived under the scaffolding on the sidewalk of a Church. His story was very touching to Chris who never forgot it. He was the son of a pastor down South. He decided that he was going to go on his own and travel up to New York City as a young man.

SPIRITUAL WARFARE BEGINS

Unfortunately, James was introduced to crack which was widespread here during the 80's. He became dependent upon it and like many others it destroyed his life. So much to the point where he could never hold a job and the streets became his home. Chris would share the Bible with him every night, eat together and talk about life. He knew that sometimes it is just as important to let someone know they're not alone in this world and that's what he wanted him to know every night that he worked.

One night, Chris was kept inside to work the phones and was disappointed as well as worried that James would think he wasn't coming to visit tonight. To Chris's surprise, one of the rookies that he was driving around on previous shifts, walked up to Chris. He said, "I bought some food tonight and brought it over to James."

Chris was amazed and honestly filled with joy to hear this. Something started to happen that he never planned on or really entered his mind. He started to notice that some of the toughest cops he had ever known were now opening up as well at times. Giving of themselves to people out there in ways they were not asked to on this job.

It was drilled into their heads time after time, that when you see someone sitting outside in a park at 2 am they're only up to no good. Chris started to realize that maybe they're just going through something just as he did on the fateful night in Long Beach only months ago.

One night, he saw a guy sitting on a bench in a Harlem Park. This is an illegal activity as per city rules and Police officers are to either issue a summons or use their best judgment to handle the situation. As Chris began to talk with this young man, he was explaining to Chris that he just got in a very bad argument with his girlfriend and needed to clear his head. Chris's partner kept a close eye on him from the vehicle as he was not too far away. As Chris got to speak with him more, they began to fellowship, and Chris felt the urge to speak with him about resolving the argument. This was a common recurrence in his own life over the years and felt he knew the answer to share with the man. It was as if God fixed him and was now using him in those situations to help others.

The man looked at Chris and said, "I have never met a cop like you, you are on fire."

Chris walked back to the vehicle and told his partner everything's fine and explained the situation. As Chris was about to pull off, he heard a door open, and looked over. His partner had exited the vehicle and was walking towards the young man in the park. A lot of things were running through Chris's mind as he was trying to understand what he was doing. This was a very tough cop who never had a lot to say unless it was important and somebody you didn't want to mess with.

As he walked up to the guy, Chris could see him reach out his hand and give him an unopened bottle of water to drink. There was a very pleasant exchange as he walked back to the vehicle and sat down. He didn't say much but Chris just stared at him with a smiling grin. He must have known Chris was burning a hole in the side of his face with the stare.

His partner looked over and said, "What? He looked thirsty," as he smiled back.

These were the most enjoyable years of Chris's time at the NYPD. Life began to take on a whole new meaning for him and he couldn't be more excited to be a cop. He felt he worked with some of the best and most caring cops in the NYPD.

As Chris began to experience this whole new world, he soon found out there was also another side, a darker side that he was going to be subjected to. The only way to understand that something is good, is to see that there is also evil. Chris was about to come face to face with the author of Evil as it would soon be searching for him.

It was 2 am on a cold midnight shift. The call comes over to Chris's unit that night, 32 John.

As dispatch puts over the call, "32 John, Eighth and West 147 Street. Caller states, there is a woman on the roof and about to jump."

Chris's unit as well as the others raced to the location. Midnight sectors were a very tight crew. The overnights, as well as being dangerous, were always short-staffed. Most of the sectors worked day tours, so if a midnight sector was in trouble, your life would be in the hands of those few cops working. Everyone showed up to a big job such as this.

Chris, his partner, and the rest of the midnight sectors ran up the stairs to the roof of the building. Chris was the first to the roof door. As he opened the door, he saw a disheveled looking woman with long scraggly hair, pacing back and forth and mumbling to herself. Right away, Chris believed she was an Emotionally Disturbed Person or (EDP as classified by the NYPD) on the roof. He saw this many times as a medic. He called out to the woman, "Ma'am can I talk to you?"

SPIRITUAL WARFARE BEGINS

The woman, still pacing and looking down, replied in an angry voice, "You have nothing I want to hear."

Chris took another slow step toward her as the rest of the cops were in line behind him as to not scare the woman. Chris was attempting to stall as they waited for the emergency service unit to arrive. The emergency service unit had special training and equipment for these situations.

Feeling led in his new calling, he said something he would never have thought of before. "Ma'am, I can see you're going through something, But God can help you through it."

The woman came to a halt. She slowly looked up at Chris. This was the first time he could see her face as the moonlit sky gave just a glimpse. She stared at him and with a look that seemed to go right through. It was a look he had never seen before. She said in a strange voice, "God? God doesn't even know who you are! Who are you?"

Chris turned around to look to his partner for help. His partner was a Christian himself and saw what was happening. He gave Chris a look.

"This is all you bro, get out there," he said and smiled.

Chris and the woman exchanged words over the next few minutes until back up came and she voluntarily left with Chris, his partner, and the ambulance for the hospital. He couldn't help but wonder about what had just happened. He knew this was something different than he had experienced in the past with FDNY or the NYPD.

SPIRITUAL WARFARE BEGINS

While Chris and his partner stayed with this woman during her intake into the hospital, Chris seeing a calm in the storm decided to strike up a conversation. The woman began to explain she was a cutter. She would cut herself at times when she became angry or uncontrollable. She was never diagnosed with any mental illness, but these types of things would happen to her as they did tonight for no reason.

Chris immediately thought of the account in the Bible where Jesus approached two demon possessed men by the tombs. One of the men was said to have been always cutting himself with stones. Chris didn't know what to make of this, at that moment, but knew something he could do.

Chris asked if he could pray for her. Chris prayed out loud in the middle of the ER as his partner joined in. The result was much better when God was brought up as the woman was at peace this time.

This type of activity would amp up in the coming days as Chris would be exposed to something that would one day connect the dots for him overseas.

A few days later, Chris and his partner responded to another call concerning an Emotional Disturbed Woman. As they walked up the stairs of the apartment, behind the other cops, Chris made direct eye contact with a woman. She was a heavy set, young black woman sitting on her bed. She was sitting with her body pointing away from him as her face was turned and staring directly at him. She had a devious smirk on her face and what could only be explained as dark, eerie eyes. Again, this was not the normal look of an EDP that he has been exposed to for years. Chris sensed something was not right once again but continued in his duties.

As one of the cops that was handling the situation cuffed her up, Chris walked back and sat in the driver seat of the police car. He sat there watching his partner speaking with the parents of the young woman as she was being situated into the ambulance.

As the ambulance drove off, his partner returned to the car, sat down, and said, "You're not going to believe this one." He continued, "They're actually here staying with family. They just got in from Africa and are here for an exorcism."

Chris leaned back to his left toward the driver's window, while turning his head to his partner.

"Yeah," his partner said, "A witch doctor sent them here to do it."

Chris said, "Damn it, you should've come and told me, I would have wanted to hear that."

He read about stories in the Bible like this, but he figured they were just stories, or they don't happen in modern times. He had two strange experiences in the same week, and it was hard to let go of what he witnessed.

His partner chuckled and said, "Come on man, it's nonsense."

Chris started to wonder that if God is good and He can help us in our own lives, is the Devil being true evil, physically able to enter our world and destroy our lives? After a few minutes another call came on the radio, and it was back to work. As time went by this became a distant memory. This was still not a direction he was concerned with as he was still exploring his new life with family, Church, ministry, and work. That was his passion in life now.

Chris and Harmony finally decided to meet with the pastor of their new Church. He was going to begin counseling them in their relationship. Teaching them Biblical principles of what a relationship should look like. They were eager to learn these teachings.

It was about 5:00 p.m. as they walked into the office of the pastor. He sat there listening intently to their stories. He had begun to stare at Chris with deep focus as he spoke about the events of his life. Chris could tell as he watched the pastor that he had something to say and was about to cut in.

The pastor looking for a break in the story, said to Chris, "You remind me of a person named Joseph in the Bible. He went through a very difficult path. He was abandoned and unjustly accused of many things."

Chris just looked at him, as this obviously sparked curiosity. He had never heard or read of this Joseph in the Bible yet. He was already thinking in his head that he couldn't wait to learn this story.

The pastor went on to say, "It was God who laid out this path for him for a specific reason. Just read the story and we will talk about it."

Chris couldn't help but smile. Even though he did not understand the story yet, he at least felt a sense of encouragement.

SPIRITUAL WARFARE BEGINS

The pastor stood up and walked over to the couple. They could both see he had something specific on his mind. He stood over them and began to pray but this was no regular prayer that either of them had ever heard before. It seemed to be genuinely specific to each of their situations. Then he prayed something that changed their lives forever.

The pastor began to pray for the Holy Spirit to come into them and fill their lives. As he did this, he laid one hand on each of their heads. It seemed to Chris that he was calling down the fire of Heaven into that room. He spoke with such authority, passion, and Biblical clarity. It was just amazing. They stood up refreshed and ready to put everything they learned today into practice for their new life together.

As the couple left, Chris turned around quickly and asked, "Oh yeah, do we pay you or the secretary out front for the session?"

The pastor with a look of surprise, was taken off guard. He again realized how new they really were to Church and the Christian faith.

He said with a smile, "This is free, we would never charge to help you."

Chris was shocked. As far as he knew and the old world he was from, if you want something you pay for it. He started to feel he had a friend in this pastor. He was a good man and invested a lot of his time in both of them. Chris still credits him today as one of the most instrumental people in his life. He helped him understand his faith and stay grounded, as this new world became a reality in his life.

SPIRITUAL WARFARE BEGINS

Chris decided to call out of work that night as they both felt so at peace and refreshed. They figured they would get a nice dinner and spend the night talking about what they learned about their relationship from the pastor. Unknown to Chris at the time, the night was about to get really strange.

As they slept, Chris heard a noise. He looked over at Harmony sleeping soundly. As he sat up to look at the dark, quiet, room he could see out through the doorway. He became startled as he saw the hallway light turned on. As he was about to get out of bed to see if it was one of the kids, he was thrown down on the bed. He watched in horror as two figures jumped up in the bed on top of his legs.

He felt some type of invisible force lift his torso straight up, so he was now sitting up looking directly at what was in the room with him. As almost in slow motion one of the figures moved forward from the edge of the bed. The dark shadow of a figure left the darkness as his face was now inches from Chris's.

Before Chris could get a look, he was flipped over onto his stomach and could not move. He began to violently struggle attempting to break the hold. His head was facing Harmony but could not speak a word. He felt scared but not terrified. He was still trying to make sense of what was going on.

Suddenly the room began to materialize around him as when someone wakes from a dream. He could now move.

He thought in that moment, "A dream?"

SPIRITUAL WARFARE BEGINS

As the room began to turn into reality, he turned to his left quickly and stared at the mirror. He jumped back as he witnessed the faces of two creatures staring back through the mirror. They had small round faces and wore black hoods. He saw small black eyes, sharp teeth, with almost a jagged diagonal line separating half their faces. Then they disappeared. Chris got up from his bed, grabbed his journal and quickly drew what he saw so he would not forget.

That Sunday after Church service, Chris decided he would share his experience with one of the senior members who he had become friendly with over the past months. "I had this dream the other night that two demons attacked me while I slept. Only I don't think it was a dream."

Chris, with Harmony now by his side listening, went on to explain the nights event as the man looked on.

When Chris finished, the man looked at him with an unconcerned look. "It was probably a dream," he replied. "And honestly, why would the devil bother with you. There are more important people for him to go after," he said in a joking manner.

Chris felt embarrassed but Harmony felt anger. As they walked away, she looked back and said to Chris, "Who would say that to someone. What a jerk."

Chris on the other hand took it to heart and felt maybe he was right. The activity continued to occur sporadically, but Chris, not wanting to be humiliated, made a point of never sharing his experiences again.

About a month later, Harmony came across a different battle of her own. One morning as she woke, she was getting dressed and she noticed something strange on her body. There was a circular mark in the middle of her back. She quickly called Chris over to take a better look.

As he ran his finger over the mark, Harmony had no pain. Harmony was heavy into fitness. She ran miles every day and was always doing sit-ups. Chris, seeing how it looked like it was skin burn, chalked it up to exercise.

In the weeks to come, Harmony's physical status began to change. She became fatigued very quickly and did not have the stamina she once had. This was blamed on the tough schedule between commuting to the city and raising the children. Still no alarms went off as life moved too fast for either of them to stop.

A few nights later, Harmony woke up in the middle of the night and could not bend her fingers. Now looking for serious answers, they got up and headed to the emergency room. After many tests, no one in the hospital could diagnose the issue. Finally, one Doctor on call figured it all out. Harmony was diagnosed with Lupus. This hit both of them hard.

Harmony had to leave the Fire Department. This was a big disappointment for her since she loved helping people and now was becoming physically unable in this capacity. Now she was the one who needed taking care of.

2009 turned out to be one strange year for Chris and Harmony. The shared experiences from living out a new Christian life, a restored family, helping the homeless, new illnesses and demonic attacks. They thought of no better experience to add to that list than to become husband and wife in 2010...which they did.

CHAPTER TEN

CONNECTICUT
The Devil Inside

A few days later, Chris and Harmony returned to Connecticut. It was against the wishes of the Catholic Church, but understanding their roots in the Evangelical Church, they knew their ultimate authority in these matters was God. Chris would not bow down to the authority of man, who made an uninformed determination without speaking to him. Helping the family was their priority whether it was the Churches or not.

The politics in the Church seemed to become more of a focus than serving the hurting. Rules and regulations replaced the heart of Christ. Objections to membership or refusal to help because you did not complete this task or did something they did not agree with in the past.

This is exactly what Jesus came to abolish with the religious leaders of the first century, when he said in **MATTHEW 11:28 "Come to me, all you who are weary and burdened, and I will give you rest."**

Chris saw one major flaw in what he was witnessing, the two greatest commandments were not the concern. God was not being glorified in these actions and love for neighbor was lacking.

As soon as they entered the home, they could tell by Glenda's expression that something struck again. Tommy was away for a couple of days staying with family. Glenda led them to an area inside, not too far from the door and just outside of the den. As they walked up, they both noticed some kind of shiny gold colored substance in the area on the white tile floor.

Chris handed Harmony the camera as he bent down to take a closer look. He followed the markings as they looked like strange small footprints leading into the kitchen. It was gold glitter that began in the middle of the room and ended right before the kitchen. Chris thought this was very strange.

Glenda said, "Yes, it's glitter, but I don't have this in my house. This happened overnight, and I have no idea how it got there."

Chris asked, "So there is no way that Tommy could have done this or maybe your sister stopped by?"

Glenda replied, "Absolutely not. No one came over plus Tommy doesn't have any glitter or would play with it. Even if he did get his hands on some, I think the house would look worse than this."

Harmony agreed with a smile, "That's true. I've been through that with my girls."

Chris focused on the print in the glitter. It wasn't any kind of human footprint. It wasn't defined enough to make it out, but it had a circular type of shape. He scooped up some of the glitter as evidence and placed it in his bag.

Glenda then led them up the stairs to her guest bedroom. She walked over and pointed to a pillow lying neatly on her made up bed. Chris walked over as Glenda stepped aside to give him a complete view. As he got closer, Harmony could hear him from the door.

"Oh boy," he said.

"What is it?" Harmony asked.

"Come take a look and bring the camera."

It was a body type pillow. On the pillow were three long tears running down the middle of the pillow at a slight angle. The tear to the left was the same length as the one to the far right, but the middle tear was longer than both. Chris placed his index, middle and ring fingers in the grooves of the torn pillow. He noticed the beginning position had his middle finger higher on the pillow than his other fingers.

As he began to trace the markings downward, he couldn't help but feel as if his hand was in the shape of a claw. He stepped away as Harmony snapped a couple of pictures and took some video. Chris stared at the pillow as a couple of things bothered him about this activity more than the obvious reason that something unexplainable cut up this pillow.

There were three lines. It was well known that the Devil strikes in threes to mock the trinity of God. As well, Jesus was said to have died on the cross at 3pm. Many times, demonic activity will occur at 3am as a sign of their constant rebellion as well as to mock their Creator.

He asked Glenda, "Do you have any idea when this activity could have happened?"

She replied, "No, I found it this morning when I happened to come in the room. I'm positive though it must have happened overnight but unsure of the time."

The other thing that concerned Chris was the type of tears. Holding his hand in the air as it would look like on the pillow, he was spotted by Glenda who had a frozen look.

"Wait," she yelled. "I have some other things I was about to show you!" as she ran downstairs to get her phone.

As she quickly returned, she said, "I know you told me to keep an eye on Tommy to observe if he keeps talking about this thing. His uncle just sent me this picture last night of Tommy."

Chris looked at Harmony as if the mutilated pillow wasn't bad enough, now this. Glenda opened her phone as Chris and Harmony both gasped.

Glenda said, "Tommy was holding up both hands like you just did."

There was Tommy's uncle, smiling next to him, as Tommy stood there making large claw hands.

Chris thought to himself while looking at the uncle's smiling, clueless face, "That poor bastard has no idea what's going on."

Tommy stood there with his make-believe claw hands while showing all his teeth. He was infatuated with lions at this point. Chris couldn't imagine what was being revealed to him in this house. Even worse, was it affecting him outside the house as well now? The more the evidence piled, confirming his theory, the more furious he became that he and his wife were left on their own to deal with something as serious as a possible child possession.

Glenda slid the screen using her finger to the next video on her iPhone. It was a video of Glenda and Tommy having a conversation about Meshaw. Chris and Harmony listened to the exchange between the aunt and four year-old nephew and were horrified. To hear the description that she was seeing was almost too much for Harmony.

The following is the transcript from the video:

Tommy: "Meshaw."

Glenda: "What about him?"

Tommy: "He has a long tail."

Glenda: "Meshaw, he has a long tail?"

Tommy: "A big head."

Glenda: "A big head?"

Tommy: "Little toes."

Tommy: "He has a shield and a sword."

Glenda: "A shield and a sword?"

Tommy: "Yep."

Tommy: "Teeth"

Glenda: "And teeth?"

Tommy: "Sharp teeth."

Tommy: "He's a boy."

Glenda: "So, he's a boy?"

Tommy: "Mmm, what's he doing in our house?"

Glenda: Yes, what is he doing inside our house, do you know why he is in our house?"

Tommy: "Yeah, yeah."

Tommy: "He has black eyes."

Tommy: "He wants to come inside, that's why my belly hurts."

When the video stopped, everyone sat there in silence for a moment. Chris stood up and walked towards the window, rubbing the back of his head trying to process the information. Harmony just sat there looking into space. Chris turned and looked at her knowing something else was bothering her.

Chris asked politely, "Glenda would you mind giving us a couple of minutes while we discuss some things?"

As she walked downstairs, Chris sat on the bed next to Harmony.

He asked, "What's going on?"

She replied, "It's fine."

CONNECTICUT - THE DEVIL INSIDE

Chris asked again, "Tell me, what?"

Harmony replied, "Watching little Tommy on the video gave me some flashbacks to the case in New Hampshire."

Harmony said, "Hearing his voice shift even just a little and what might be happening again, reminded me what happened on the couch when I was in the middle of interviewing Peter."

Chris, hearing this, felt terrible that he didn't pick up on this right away. Harmony went through a traumatic experience that only a few have most likely encountered in a lifetime. Chris was the one who always felt responsible, as this once again became a horrible reminder to them both of what might be occurring.

Not long before this Connecticut case took place, there was New Hampshire. One evening, Chris received a call from his good friend from Church, Dan.

He said, "Do you remember Stephen from Church? He's here with me, he needs your help with the ministry you do."

Stephen was someone Chris remembered very well. They bonded many years earlier as Stephen was one of the few that would come out on the streets with him and Dan to evangelize. Just as with this ministry, pure street evangelism is a very lonely and dangerous ministry at times. You can find the strongest friendships with brothers and sisters out there that can last a lifetime. Stephen was a solid Christian and had a huge heart for loving people which was an example for Chris in a way to make him a better person.

They haven't spoken for years and when Chris heard he needed help he was surprised.

Chris responded, "Of course, put him on."

Chris said, "What's up Stephen? Long time."

With his voice a bit shaken, he replied, "Well, I just got back from a friend's house who moved to New Hampshire, and I feel like I just came from the pit of hell."

Chris said, "Ok, so the answer is not good, got it. That would have been fine."

Stephen gave a chuckle as he knew Chris was trying to make him relax.

Chris said, "Just start from the beginning and tell me what's going on."

Stephen went on to tell some story. He told Chris that a couple of days ago he went to stay with this friend. He knew right away that something was different about him. He wasn't himself and things had not gone well for him over the past couple of months.

He said, "The last night I was there, my friend Pete and I were driving back from dinner. It was a windy two-lane highway. He began to drive erratic as he couldn't focus on the road."

I asked him, "What's going on?"

He replied, "There is something controlling me. I can't stay on the road."

I asked him, "Does it want to kill us?"

He said without hesitation, "Yes!"

"I grabbed the wheel and yelled at him to put the brake on. I drove home as he couldn't understand what had happened. It was as if he was a different person a moment earlier." Stephen continued in the story. "When we were home that night, I was up in my room packing up some things. Suddenly I heard a loud guitar playing downstairs and what sounded like a few voices singing. I thought Pete put heavy metal music on the radio. When I went down the stairs, I saw it was Pete playing the guitar and singing in a strange voice. It was creepy."

He told me, "I don't know, it feels like my hands move on their own and I can play songs. Pretty cool right?"

Stephen continued to watch for a few more moments. He noticed how he was carelessly hitting the strings, but the music sounded in tune with the rock song he recognized.

Stephen told Chris, "That was it for me. I went upstairs, closed the door, and put on Christian music."

"I heard what you and your wife do, can you help him?" Stephen asked.

One week later, Chris, Harmony and Stephen headed to New Hampshire. They decided to take Stephen along since he had a strong friendship with the victim. Chris never took anyone along with them on a case, but he thought it would make things smoother at the location. Plus having one more Christian around that is willing to go? Well, that's never a bad idea.

Chris could see Stephen through the rear-view mirror as he looked out the window in the back seat. It was obvious Stephen was tense about a couple of things. He was heading back to Hell as he saw it and that he was going with these people who were involved in a ministry he couldn't understand.

Before leaving, Stephen received the blessing from his own pastor, Pastor Tom, and longtime friend of Chris to go with them. He gave the strict warning to listen to whatever Chris tells you to do. His entire Church was aware of the situation and prayed over Stephen before leaving.

Chris and Harmony became outcasts of surrounding Long Island Churches since being called into this type of ministry. Chris, once held up as a lead evangelist in the Church, was now looked on as dangerous. Members of surrounding Churches alerted him that a pastor was spreading rumors around that he and his wife are crazy as congregations were told to stay away from them.

Once again, gossip spread as no one personally inquired about what they were actually doing. This hurt Chris greatly. Pastor Tom was the only pastor who publicly supported him in this ministry. He continually offered Biblical wisdom as he was delighted to see Chris's evolution from street evangelism to house evangelism.

Peter greeted them at the door. He was a respected Cardiovascular Surgeon in the state, who retired a few months back. This home was going to be his retirement home to live out his years. He was a very mild-mannered man who spoke very eloquently as you might expect from a Surgeon.

Chris and Harmony conducted an on-camera interview on the back deck. The house was in total seclusion by the surrounding fields, so privacy was not an issue. Peter went on to answer questions regarding the incidents, past medical history, and anything else they needed, all with grace. He was thrilled that they came from New York in such a short time, and he was willing to volunteer whatever was needed to fix this terrible issue.

Peter explained that since moving in he has developed many illnesses and injuries to his back and knees. Recently as he was standing in the doorway to the basement, he was pushed by some type of invisible force. If he didn't grab the railing at the last second, he would have tumbled down the cellar steps.

Chris decided to switch gears and ask him about the personality changes that Stephen mentioned. Chris asked, "What can you tell me about that scary ride home from dinner with Stephen last week?"

Peter replied, "Most of it I can't remember. Just that I couldn't control myself."

Chris continued on to the next subject before Peter had time to see where he might be going. "I hear you're a pretty good guitar player. How long have you been playing?" Chris asked.

Peter replied, "Honestly not long. I collect some but have not really had any formal teaching."

Chris said, "Stephen here says you sounded pretty good the other night."

Peter responded, "I was telling him, I feel like I can just play, so I do. I don't understand it myself."

Peter began to sob, "Thank you for coming. I'm dying here and I know something evil is here trying to kill me or take me over."

Chris was very concerned about hearing this as one of the signs of possession listed by Catholic Exorcists is the "knowing of secret knowledge" or "hidden things." He suspected this might fall into this category and combined it with the other night.

Not to mention, he recalled that one of the first things he remembered as a medic was to listen to the patient. If he tells you he feels like he's dying, believe him. Peter was saying the same thing in the spiritual sense. Chris knew there's a good chance they were looking at a possession.

Still, his first inclination was to attempt to debunk the theory or look for some kind of rational answer. As they walked around the home, they entered a room that sent the electromagnetic field reader spiking. As he looked around for wires or some type of electric source for the answer, the metal plate in his left arm began to feel as if it was heating up with numbness. At least he knew there was an energy source in the room and the meter was not misreading.

Over the past year, Chris discovered that in many cases, he would feel little shocks in the plates that were housed in both forearms for the past three decades. It could best be described as if something got too close to an electrified fence. After a while, combining it with other evidence gathered on scenes, he was amazed to find that the plates in his forearms became his most reliable tool.

Over time, he came to believe that one of the worst moments in his life, having metal plates which ended any chance of a baseball career, may have been some Divine intervention.

When Harmony heard the device, she entered the room and Chris immediately let her know the room was not good.

Chris said, "My arm is on fire."

She knew exactly what that meant from past cases. When he used that phrase, she knew something was going on.

Curiously she walked to Chris and replied, "Really?"

Chris moved towards her, shoving her out of the room quickly as they both moved back to the hallway. "Get out! Get out!" he yelled.

After the couple completed their preliminary investigation around the entire property, which took several hours, they met back with Peter. Chris wanted to know more about this one room where he felt the energy. Peter told him that among many things, there was an antique desk he acquired from an auction house. Chris understood he needed to go back and take a closer look.

Chris and Peter entered the room as Chris began to look through the drawers for any clues. As he opened the soft green carpeted drawers, Chris began to ask if the desk was purchased empty or if there were any items attached to it?

Peter said, "Oh you know what? I can't believe I forgot to tell you this."

Chris dropped his head. If he could count how many times he had heard that. It was common for people to forget a major detail or to even think it wasn't a big deal. Chris remembered one case, where he was helping a "Christian" who was having wild activity in her home. As he inspected the home, he found a Voodoo doll in a basket on her dresser.

When he questioned her on it, she said, "They helped me make it when I went to New Orleans. Is there something wrong with that?"

Chris turned from looking at the desk as Peter led him downstairs to the fireplace in the den.

"See that?" Peter said, pointing to a pile of ashes in the fireplace. He continued, "That was a bunch of Tarot cards that I found in the dresser after I got it home."

Chris replied, "And you burned them?"

"Well not me" Peter explained. "A Christian friend of mine came over after I told her what I found. She took them and burned them."

Chris replied, "Ok, well that was not a good idea. Was that before or after the activity began around you and your home?"

Peter lifted his head slightly, looking at the corner of the ceiling and said, "Come to think of it, it was before. Actually, not too long before."

Chris explained, "So it looks like we may have nailed down the invitation or access point into your home. By your friend burning the cards, if an entity was attached to them, it might have been set free to run wild."

Peter agreed, "That makes sense since this all basically began after she did that."

Chris explained further, "We don't know why they were left there? Either by accident or on purpose? To bring harm to the new owner or for other use? One thing I know, whatever was attached to those cards, must go."

As the case turned out, it was one of the greatest gifts Chris and Harmony ever experienced in this ministry. In the end, after blessing the home and extensive prayer over Peter, he was healed of every ailment he had and came to know the LORD. Something that amazed Stephen so much that he spread the word throughout Long Island afterwards.

But Harmony came face to face with the Demon before they reached that place of victory. As Stephen was showing Chris something outside on the property, Harmony began to interview Peter a little more. She was asking in more detail regarding his past medical and mental health history, which he was more than happy to do.

Harmony was now alone in the room with Peter. She sat on the couch with him in the open den in the front of the house. There was a large window looking out to the front yard, as she saw Chris clearly on the porch looking around.

She began asking about any type of medications he may be taking that can cause hallucinations. She asked in detail about mental health issues in the past as well. Harmony knew it was very important to rule out any other causes for his personality shift if they were going to ask for future help from the Church. Peter confirmed it was not the cause of any medications or history.

She then explained, "If there is something attaching itself to you or oppressing you, it has not revealed itself yet. We need to gather a little more information and since you are being affected by this so strongly, we may need to bring in a bigger team to help, maybe the Church."

There was a pause for 3 or 4 seconds. The very approachable and welcoming person she was sitting next to seemed to change his demeanor. He slowly turned his head towards Harmony with a look that paralyzed her.

Peters voice turned from a warm, helpful voice to a deep whisper as he said, "That makes no freaking sense to me."

Harmony sensing something was going horribly wrong and caught off guard, as she gave off a nervous giggle.

Peter said in a continued low sarcastic voice, "What are you talking about? Do you know something I don't know?"

"Listen honey, I don't need your help. Thank you for coming, you can leave."

This well-mannered man who spoke nothing but respect all day was now a different person. He spoke in this steady, slow voice using sarcasm, curses, and belittling comments to shake her up.

Harmony trying her best to hide her fear, attempted to de-escalate the situation in a professional manner, said, "We just want you to be ok and get you the best help possible."

He replied, "Listen, my brother is a Catholic Priest, I'm all about God."

As Harmony attempted to speak, she was abruptly cut off.

Peter said, "It isn't going to happen."

Harmony stared past Peter, through the window at Chris, hoping for any look from him into the room. Just one look and she could wave him in or grab his attention.

Peter spoke again to bring her attention back to him. "I'll take care of you guys and pay you. Thank you."

Harmony said, "We don't want your money, we don't charge. We help because we want to."

She could sense whatever and whoever was speaking was now looking to create an obstacle to helping Peter get free.

Acting way out of character bouncing on the couch and laughing like a child, he replied sarcastically, "That's great. Here is the counselor trying to help."

Just then, the screen door opened, and Chris walked back into the room. The room came to a dead stop, and it went quiet. He could feel and see the tension immediately. Harmony looked shaken up as Peter just sat there as if nothing happened.

Peter said in a jolly voice, "Ok, let's go out to supper!"

Chris looked at Harmony as she gave him a look that told him something was wrong. "What happened?" asked Chris.

Peter replied, "Well, your wife and I had a heart to heart that didn't go well. We had some disagreements that weren't that big of a deal."

Harmony cut in and gave an account of everything that had just happened to bring Chris up to speed. Peter said, "That's not what I told you, come on."

Peter was now trying to persuade Chris that nothing that his wife said happened that way and that she was even being rude when they spoke. As Harmony went to respond, Chris jumped in politely and took control of the situation. He calmed everyone down as he decided that was enough for today and they would head back to the hotel for the night.

When they were packing up all the gear, Chris noticed a voice recorder from an earlier part of the investigation. It was accidentally left in that room and was recording the entire conversation. When they went back to the hotel and listened to the recording, Chris was mortified at what he heard. He was sick to his stomach that he left Harmony alone in that situation and vowed to never get so caught up on a case that she would be left alone again. Harmony has been traumatized by what she witnessed firsthand since the event.

Chris stood up from the bed in Glenda's room as Harmony sat there quietly.

He looked at her and said, "Do you feel up to this? I totally get it if you don't."

"Of course," she replied.

Chris said, "I have done it alone in the past (referring to the actual house blessing). You don't have to worry, I got this."

Harmony stood up and said, "I'm fine, I just needed a minute."

The two walked out of the room and turned towards the door that opens into the attic entrance.

They brought a large black duffle bag with them which contained the blessing kit. Chris opened the door slowly and saw that the square wooden cover for the attic opening was dislodged. They looked with surprise but not shocked as this was par for the course in this case.

Chris looked up, put one hand on the ladder and said, "I guess he wants to say hello. Let's finish this."

CHAPTER ELEVEN

MINISTRY
2009-2018

Over the next 9 years, God would lead Chris and Harmony into many different ministries in many different areas. After a while, it became apparent that they would find themselves outside the walls of the Church on their own. They understood that the Church had responsibilities to those coming in, being that they themselves were those same people. But they also understood that there was a big responsibility outside as well, delivering the message of the Gospel.

They were committed to bringing this same message that they received that beautiful Sunday morning to those who might never make it to a service like that. They knew people deserved to at least hear the truth and decide for themselves. This was between God and the person, just as it was with Chris and Harmony. They were just called to deliver His message and leave the results up to Him.

God began to call Chris to lead the family in this new direction. The interesting thing was that Chris was basically an introvert. He wasn't much for the public scene and the thought of public speaking in front of large groups would make him sick. That was not in his DNA.

The Ministry of evangelism started off with a small crowd but not an easy one. One morning, soon after becoming a Christian, Chris decided it was time to share what had happened to him, with his father.

His Italian and Catholic upbringing going back generations would make this a foreign message to his father. He wasn't devout by any means, but his father never missed making the sign of the cross as they drove by a Catholic Church growing up. He always wore his gold necklace with a medallion showing the head of Christ wearing his crown of thorns. To get to the point, his first opportunity to share the Gospel did not go well.

Another time, he woke up and began to create little messages about Jesus to share with people. He felt he wanted to share with Long Beach. The boardwalk would be the perfect place on the weekend. Chris, with the help of his wife, made many flyers as they would put them up all over the town. The flyer read,

"ATTENTION MEN: SATURDAY 9AM at the Long Beach Boardwalk with Chris. Let's talk about Jesus and have some breakfast."

As the week approached, Chris began to have second thoughts.

"What am I nuts?" He thought.

He needed confirmation from God before he went down there and made a complete fool of himself in front of the whole town. Fear gripped him as the reality of what he was about to do and the public perception flooded his thoughts.

He got down on his knees and began to ask God for a sign. "Listen God, I need to know this is You and I'm not

MINISTRY 2009-2018

out of my mind. I need something big. Something where I will know it is You. Show me a big cross in the sky. Please let me know this is You."

As the week went by, Chris saw nothing. He looked up every day hoping to see something that could at least confirm that he was not losing it. As Saturday morning arrived there was still no big cross in the sky. Chris was disappointed but relieved. He figured that he wasn't being called to do anything but at least he didn't have to make a fool of himself either. He sat out on the front porch with his son Jake, as they had a bowl of cereal together.

It was around 8:30 a.m. on this beautiful Saturday morning. Blue skies for miles and the smell of salt from the beach once again filled the air of this beach town. Chris was sitting facing the house, as he was looking at repairs that might be needed. Little Jake was enjoying his breakfast, his eyes wandered up and down the block watching people begin to head to the boardwalk.

Suddenly, Jake's voice broke the silence. "Wow, that's the biggest cross I have ever seen!"

Chris turned quickly towards Jake to see him pointing directly overhead.

Chris was amazed and in disbelief at the same time. He threw his bowl down to the table and ran off into the house, screaming for Harmony.

He stopped mid run and dropped down to his knees as he thanked God. He looked at the clock, 8:35! "Lord, I gotta run!" he said in a joyful panic.

Harmony hearing all the commotion came out. When she heard what had happened, she started shouting as well, "Go, you have to go!"

She began to throw his backpack at him as he headed to the door, hopping around as he put on his sneakers. As he was about to leave, he stopped for a moment to stare at that Cross in the sky. His eyes began to fill as he thought to himself, "God sent me that. That was just for me."

He grabbed a camera from the living room and snapped a picture as to never forget one of the first miracles he experienced with God. It is still on his wall today as a reminder, that God hears prayers.

As he ran to the store on the corner with only minutes before the meeting at the location, he filled his bag with bagels and juice. As he walked around the boardwalk, Chris did not meet one person that morning. He didn't speak to anyone as the opportunity never arose.

He sat on the bench overlooking the water trying to figure out what had just happened. "I just spent a ton of money that I don't have and I'm sitting here with a breakfast for ten men," he thought.

So, he pulled out a bagel, juice, and his Bible. Someone had to eat it. As he read the Psalms and ate, he realized something. This was never about meeting anyone.

This was for him. God was testing him to see if he would follow through and go, while showing Chris that he can depend on Him. Although Chris sat there alone by himself on a bench that morning, he was never alone and more importantly, he knew it. That morning was for God and Chris to get to know each other. Saturday was a good day.

The result of that event brought about the Ministry "Seek and Save Outreach," formed by the couple. The name was founded on **LUKE 19:10: *"For the Son of Man came to seek and to save the lost."***

The Gospel was shared all over Long Island as the children even became involved as they would help create family events around it. One time, on a road trip back to Michigan, they stopped at rest stops along the way to hand out water and CDs with a spoken Gospel message from Chris. The kids were learning firsthand about the importance of a bigger world than just their own.

As Chris grew in the Church, he began to teach and preach during Bible studies and men's groups. He would take the men out after study and show them how to live it out and speak it to complete strangers. Chris was now being groomed to become a pastor.

As his rotating work schedule at the precinct began to become an obstacle to Sunday service, he decided he needed a change. He applied to the department for a religious exemption and to exchange other days for Sundays off to be able to go to Church. He was quickly denied. He was told Christians do not need a specific day to worship.

As a blessing, the admin office in the precinct who handles these types of transactions got wind of this. The Lieutenant in charge was very understanding and began to personally change his shifts so he could attend his Church. He was moved by her concern, and it was something he never forgot.

Not too long after, as Chris was still working the midnight shift, an opportunity arose inside the precinct. The Lieutenant offered Chris a position to come off the street and to help take care of the daily maintenance of the building. Chris was caught off guard. This never entered his mind as he loved being out with his partner in the streets.

She explained to him that it came to mind because he would have a regular five-day work week and weekends off. He could now go to Church regularly. Chris was left with a big decision. He would basically leave patrol, but he would gain a lot coming inside. He would consistently have time with family and Church, what could be more important.

After speaking with his wife, he made the move. He wasn't sure it would be the best move for the precinct since he was not close to what you would call a handy man... as they would soon find out.

Soon after, God began to open more doors for Chris and Harmony. A pastor from a nearby Church called Chris to preach Sunday sermons with him and some other men at a nursing home in Medford, Long Island. It was an amazing experience as he saw the excitement the residents had for visitors every Sunday. This gave Chris another idea.

With the permission of the pastor, Chris decided to visit the facility once a week as well. He couldn't think of any better person to bring than his wife. Together, they would go visit the elderly, listen to their stories, and pray with them. Many loving relationships were starting. Chris shared the Gospel and Harmony, the caregiver, helped in so many areas ranging from social work issues to intercession with other family members.

Chris, now looking to become a pastor, began to focus on Biblical education. He began online seminary courses as well as pastor credentialing for the Assemblies of God Christian organization. Wanting to learn as much as possible he learned the original language of the New Testament, Koine Greek to find the most accurate translation to English.

He also became an accomplished Apologist, being able to defend the Gospel against opposing views. One trip took Chris and Harmony to join other Christians in Washington D.C. Chris was one of many to debate atheists in a public fashion on the steps of the Lincoln Memorial at the National "Reason Rally."

Also, he was now working in sunlight for the first time since the late 90's. He began to take the train to work. He saw very busy Times Square with probably thousands of people from all different countries passing through daily. To him, that was evangelizing the world. He could share the same message that changed his life, right there in the middle of Times Square and it would be as if he was sharing it with the entire world.

He began to hand out little messages or Bible tracks and speak to people as he waited for his train. One time he was approached by a Muslim man who worked for the sight-seeing tour bus service. He approached Chris to hear what he was saying and handing out. After a very nice talk, the man was so moved by the message that he took half of Chris's stack and began to hand them out with him. Chris never saw anything like this before as he rushed to call his friend, Pastor Tom, with the incredible news.

Something else caught his eye on these walks to the train. Something that was a first passion for him and his wife, that he felt he was leaving behind in all these new ventures... The homeless. Chris saw the streets lined with homeless people. From the elderly to young people, Veterans to teens. It was heartbreaking for Chris, from his prior experience working this ministry at work knew that they all had a story. He was going to listen.

He heard many stories from young military veterans being denied benefits and counseling which he found criminal. He met one young man in particular who suffered a brain trauma in Iraq. As a result, he developed neurological as well as psychological issues. He was not able to receive the medical insurance he deserved and found himself with a substance abuse problem on the streets to alleviate the issues. Many of these stories began to overwhelm him as he took them home to Harmony.

One day as he walked the city streets looking for someone to help, he ran into a couple of older gray hair guys, Jim and Mike. These men were enjoying some canned beer in brown paper bags, sitting on their cardboard boxes under the scaffolding on the corner of Eighth Avenue and 34th Street. Chris decided to stop and say hello.

The men were very friendly as they invited him to sit down on the cardboard with them. They began to share stories together as the sidewalks were filled with commuters making their way across the street to catch a train. As Chris sat with them, one of the passersby, laid food down at the feet of the hungry men as they gave a thank you. Chris smiled but then was surprised when she also laid a sandwich down at his feet as well.

The men laughed with a hysterical cackle as they said, "Welcome Chris, you're one of us."

Chris chuckled back as he looked down at his old shorts and worn t-shirt he wore home from the precinct. As they continued to speak a group of four or five people joined under the scaffolding in a kind of a circle. It was obvious to Chris that they all knew each other and spoke often.

One of the women, began to share a funny story of how she pickpocketed one of the tourists by 57th Street. She joked as she talked about it as if they can make a killing over there today. Chris was caught off guard by the direction of the story as he was only in Christian mode at that time.

Just then he got a strange feeling as one of the much younger guys kept staring at him. He knew this guy didn't want him there. Chris was an outsider. The young guy spoke up in the group, "Who's this guy?" as he looked directly at Chris.

The rest of the group looked at Chris as the woman stopped telling her story. He felt a little twinge in his stomach that arises when you know something uncomfortable is about to happen, and it did.

Jim, half in the bag, spoke up in Chris's defense. "No, this is Chris, he's from a Church. He's a good guy."

Chris, in a state of panic, kept hearing a voice in his head, "Why did I tell them? Don't say it Jim, don't say it Jim."

And then...

Jim said in a loud voice, "He's a cop!"

Jim said it. Chris clenched his fist as he was waiting for someone to charge at him.

Instead, the newcomers said, "I'm out of here," and dispersed as fast as they showed up.

With that Chris did the same. Laughing at himself, he knew he learned another life lesson. Don't be a moron.

As the Times Square Ministry grew, he brought in more people to help. His kids were all teenagers now with even Sarah entering college. Back home, Harmony and the rest of the family would make food and packets of warm weather gear as winter approached.

Chris remembered a nice memory when his daughter, Sarah, and her boyfriend met him in the city to help hand out the items. It moved him to see such young adults opening their hearts to complete strangers as the day went on. In the beginning they would stand behind Chris as he approached those sitting on the sidewalks. By the end of the day, each of them, without prompting would walk up to those in need and hand out a package with a "God Bless."

As summer came around, God was continuing to move in Chris's life. As he sat in the backyard one afternoon spending time meditating on all that's happened and all they have accomplished in ministry over a nine-year period, he realized something. He was not to be a pastor. That was not his calling. His ministry was evangelism outside the walls of the Church.

At that moment, something happened in that backyard with God. Chris felt something else in his heart. Something he never felt before or even thought about. He was feeling a need to help in a greater way. In his understanding, what else could there be? He had a fulltime Job in NYC as a cop, a wife with Lupus, and four kids to care for. He was doing what he thought was as much as humanly possible in his position.

Just then he heard a voice. Not an audible voice, but a voice that went straight to his heart. The Holy Spirit, just as He has done many times throughout the years directing his path, spoke one word... **AFRICA.**

CHAPTER TWELVE

OUT OF AFRICA

It's 2018 as Chris was sitting on his back porch in the yard. They had just purchased a home back in his childhood neighborhood two years earlier. He wanted the peace of the quiet suburbs again which have less traffic and much bigger yards to enjoy as a family. He watched the sun shining down, growing the healthy green grass, as the picket fences were lined with mulch, bushes, and colorful plants that Harmony had planted.

As he sat high on the porch, he looked to his left and could see into his neighbor's yard. There was Richie, his retired neighbor, tending to his yard as he did on most days. He must have been in his late seventies but could have easily passed for sixty. Twenty-five-year-old kids had nothing on this man when it came to staying active.

He could be seen in the mornings bringing in a neighbor's garbage pail or clearing out someone's driveway with his powerful snow blower after a storm. Many times, as Richie was cutting his front lawn with his ride on mower, he would drive onto Chris's property and cut his as well. That's the kind of person he was. After the passing of his father in 2016, Chris saw him as a father figure and was grateful to have moved next to that family.

Chris looked back towards his own yard and pondered what he had just heard in his head. Africa?

Really? He began to search on his iPhone and was taken with the poverty and the great need over on that side of the world. He walked into the house to share this with Harmony. Chris had always thought outside the box when it came to ministry, but even he knew this was not only outside the box but borderline medical evaluation territory. He was sure this was going to be shut down and rightly so.

Harmony was cleaning when Chris walked in. "Hey honey, what do you think if I traveled to Africa to help over there?" he asked, catching her off guard.

He knew it was not the typical way to ask something of this magnitude but wanted to see a genuine first reaction.

"Africa? Why Africa?" She responded with a surprised but understanding look. She continued to clean as Chris followed her around the home. She knew Chris has come up with interesting ideas over the years and really was not shocked anymore by his thoughts.

He replied, "Well honestly, I was sitting out back, praying and asking God, what's next? You know I have been feeling something bigger lately for whatever reason. I felt He wants me to go to Africa."

Harmony now stopped what she was doing. She could tell Chris was serious and understood how sensitive he was to hearing God's direction. Over the past decade, God has led them into many areas that would seem out of anyone's comfort zone. She knew she had to take this on a serious level.

She looked at him and said, "Obviously I know you're going to pray on this but if God is calling you to Africa, who am I to get in the way?"

As Chris went to work on this new mission, things began to fall right into place. A friend of his in ministry connected him with an organization in Rwanda that created a Christian school in a remote village. After speaking with them, he would need a total of $1,500 for the trip. It may not have seemed like a lot to some people, but Chris knew it would have put his family in a hole. That wasn't fair to them.

He spoke with Pastor Tom regarding a plan he had come up with. He asked the pastor to pray on this but to not tell a single soul. It was going to be only him, Harmony and Chris praying for the money to come through for his Africa trip without putting strain on his family. There was to be no asking for donations or anything like that. This was to be his confirmation from God and besides, he knew God was in control of everything and did not want to expend any energy on convincing others to give to something God had called him to do.

It was a Sunday when this began. Pastor Tom doing his part, while every chance Chris had, he would pray specific scriptures he had placed inside the cover of his Bible. Scriptures that spoke to him on God's authority, love, and faithfulness to His children. Scriptures he reads today in the battle against the Devil because of this one event.

It was two days later on this Tuesday evening in September. Chris was watching TV when an unknown number called in. He would never pick up a number he didn't recognize in the past. It was just something you grew accustomed to as a cop. Tonight, for whatever reason, he picked up.

It was the mortgage company that handled his father's home two years earlier when he passed. Chris and his sister had to basically hand the home over to them after it was declared that he had too many liens against it. Something they were both sad to see happen to their childhood home.

The woman began to explain, that they needed a signature from him and his sister to perform some legal transaction. Chris was not interested in hearing anymore since they basically gave them weeks to clear out any family items before they took ownership. As he listened, he contemplated just hanging up and going back to his show, when she said something that caught his ear.

She said, "We would pay you and your sister something if you would just come down here and sign your name."

That was a different story. Who would turn that down. Even if it was a couple of bucks, it would be something.

"Sure," he replied.

She said happily, "Great. We came up with a number but you and your sister, Nicole, will have to split it. We are going to pay out $3,000 and your half will be $1,500."

Chris heard it but didn't believe it. "Did you say I will get $1,500?" he asked.

"Yes, we talked about it yesterday and felt that was a fair number for a signature."

As he hung up the phone, he ran to the bedroom to tell Harmony what had just happened. She was surprised as well. They haven't heard a thing for two years regarding the home and tonight a call. He looked at her as he knew she wasn't processing the magnitude of that number.

"Harmony, that's the price for the entire trip to Africa," he said as he was bursting inside.

She replied, "Wow, that's right."

Chris had a moment where he contemplated using the money to help the family. Though he knew it should be for the trip, that little voice was telling him that his family could use it with the bills.

Harmony, as if the correct voice was coming through said, "Well, I guess you're going to Africa."

Chris sat down in the kitchen made some arrangements and ordered the plane ticket from JFK airport to Rwanda. It was now getting late, and Chris headed to bed where Harmony was sound asleep. Now lying in the peace and quiet of his mind, he recapped what had just happened.

God had come through as he always has but it was something more than that. It was in these times; Chris would see God as a real Father. He was in awe of thinking that God was even mindful of him. That was the biggest blessing as far as he was concerned. As he drifted off to sleep, the reality of his decision flooded his mind and gripped him with sudden fear.

Holy Crap! I'm going to Africa.

During the next week, Chris, wanting to understand the history of where he was heading, started to research. He knew of certain major events that took place in Rwanda a few decades earlier but never really looked closely.

It was a devastating story. Named by some, a "Rwandan genocide when 800,000 to one million people were brutally slaughtered in a massacre that lasted only 100 days in 1994.[1]

It was a state led mass killing that targeted an ethnic group called the Tutsis.[2]

The killings were mostly carried out by fellow citizens of a different ethnic group called the Hutus. The two groups had long standing issues that finally came to a head after the assassinations of Rwandan President Habyarimana and Burundian President Ntaryamira who were both Hutus.[3]

He read how family lines were decimated and about the psychological trauma that survivors were still dealing with today. That was the area which concerned Chris most, as he prepared for the trip. He knew he was heading into a country that experienced a horrific event so incomprehensible that he didn't know if he was ready emotionally for what he was about to see.

1,2,3. World Vision.org https://www.worldvision.org/disaster-relief-news-stories/1994-rwandan-genocide-facts

OUT OF AFRICA

A couple of weeks later, Chris headed to Africa on his own and had no idea what he was about to experience. For him, it would be a series of life-changing events one after the other, that would change the ministry as well as himself forever.

When Chris arrived in Rwanda, it was if though he landed in a different world from distant New York City that he left 22 hours earlier. He was picked up by the CEO of the school, Jason Peters. Jason was very respected in the Christian world. He was not only in charge of the Christian school but was a Chaplain in the United States Air Force. This, among other international ministries he served in earlier years, was someone Chris was looking forward to learning from.

As Chris saw him standing outside the terminal, Chris excitedly pointed at him, like they were already old friends in this first meeting. They had an instant bond just as two brothers in Christ do at times. The two of them left the airport and headed to the village in the mountains.

The streets were busy as they left the city area. What seemed like dozens of motor bikes filled the roadways as tourists could be seen holding on to the bike operators. Jason explained this was the method of transportation for the city's taxi service. As the paved road turned to dirt roads, Chris had the sense they were getting closer to the village.

The gray pickup began to bounce up and down as the ride quickly changed from smooth roads to uneven grooves in the dirt. School kids could be seen walking on either side of the road as they left the school and headed back to their little homes on the hill. Chris was immediately taken in by them as they would wave at each other as the truck drove by.

As they pulled through these massive black metal gates, it led directly into the school grounds. The children could be seen in flocks heading out the gates as parents were waiting. Out front was a security guard 24/7. Everything for the duration of Chris's stay could be located inside these gates as the sleeping quarters, food, and school were all safely inside this compound.

As nice as it felt to be in such a secure location in the mountains, it left Chris on alert, knowing there must be a reason for the safety measures.

Sleeping during the night was difficult in this new place at first as he really didn't know what to expect. Who would when they tell you to make sure you sleep inside the netting which hung from the ceiling? Mosquito, snake, lion? He didn't know what could end up there as they slept only feet from the darkness of the mountain area. One thing he knew for sure. If he ever wanted his firearm, boy it was now.

One of the first things that Chris became involved in was helping with the water issue. One day, Jason led the group out to the bottom of a steep hill. At the bottom of the hill, there were groups of little children filling up containers of water. The water was trickling out of a pipe inserted into what looked like a large rock in the hill.

There was no running water or water that dispenses from a refrigerator. This was a reality for these people. The children in these groups did not attend any school. They needed to bring water for the family up this steep hill daily to their homes in the mountain. Chris returned alone a few times during the trip to help in this area, as he was moved by the dedication and work ethic of these children. He felt bad for the kids and wanted to be a part of this.

Something else that took Chris by surprise were mirrors, or really a lack of. He noticed at some point that all the children were always reaching for his phone to look at themselves after he took their picture. That didn't surprise him as this was nothing new in America, where it seemed vanity ran wild. It was not until someone mentioned to him that most of the kids had never seen what they really looked like. They don't have cameras or even mirrors in their homes. Chris could not believe his ignorance all this time.

For most of his life, he complained about his situation. He was jealous of the rich and wanted to be wealthy as most people do. Now he felt foolish seeing how he was viewed by the people of this village. He was the rich man from America.

On Wednesday evening the Christian school was holding a big event on the school grounds. A combination of staff, children and parents numbering in the hundreds, were coming together for a night of worship, preaching and fellowship. Earlier in the day, Jason had asked Chris if he would give his testimony to the crowd tonight.

As he was called up to speak, he now got a good look for the first time at the multitudes that came out this night as he could feel his heart beating through his chest. Chris, with the microphone in hand, began his testimony of how he was brought to the Lord. The translator stood directly next to him, speaking Chris's words, sentence by sentence into the native language of Kinyarwanda. With each pause that Chris took as he waited for the translator to finish, he noticed he was going off in a different direction. When Chris had finished, he was disappointed because he didn't remember much of what he said because of the nerves. He wanted to really bring home the Gospel and right now he felt as if he blew it.

The next morning, the entire school met outside before class as the children prayed to start the day and sing some songs. As Chris was helping Jason set up some cameras and recording devices, he was approached by a man. He said he was a man in the crowd last night when Chris spoke. The man wanted to thank him, but Chris was curious as to why?

He told Chris that his testimony really touched him last night. Chris was now very interested as he couldn't remember much of what he said.

He told Chris, "I am one of the children who lost their parents in the genocide that happened here years ago. I have felt lost and alone ever since I was a child because of what happened. I was always looking for something to fill it. When I heard you saying that you felt all alone when you lost your children in divorce and your mother died, it connected with me.

Chris was listening intently as both men's eyes began to fill with water.

"When you said, that when you understood that Jesus, is the same yesterday, today and forever and He will never leave you nor forsake you, it all made sense to me. I now understand that it is only through Jesus that I will find that everlasting love and with Him, I am never alone. Thank you."

OUT OF AFRICA

The two men shook hands as they hugged. As the man walked away, Chris was in awe. He had no words to say, except, "Thank you God." He felt now he knew why he was called to Africa. What Chris didn't know was that there was another reason. One he was about to find out that would send him on a trajectory he could have never imagined.

Towards the end of the trip, Jason took Chris and a few people down the other side of the mountain into the marketplace. They hiked on foot for many miles as this was the only way down this side of the mountain. They could not have asked for a more beautiful day as the sky was blue and visibility was for miles. It was an amazing sight overlooking the land from the high altitude as they slowly descended.

As they entered the market area, they were not too hard to spot being the only white people among the hundreds walking around. They passed by large groups of people inside wooden gated areas containing dozens of goats on roped leashes. Different vendors would follow Chris and the group trying to sell families of goats as they made their way into the center of the market.

When they came around a bend, they saw another group standing around and staring at something. As Jason, Chris and the others walked by, they could see a man lying on the dirt ground in the middle of the group. As the group began dispersing, they got a good look at what was happening.

The man was writhing on the ground making a loud, high pitched, raspy sound that did not seem human to Chris. Chris took a closer look as he saw the man making a strange movement with his mouth as well. As Chris walked to the other side of the man, he could clearly see that he was biting down on his own arm attempting to drink the blood. With blood covering the man's arm, Chris looked up and they locked eyes.

The man gazed into Chris's eyes for probably only a few moments but to Chris it seemed a lifetime. He immediately realized where he had seen this look before.

He thought to himself, "These are the same eyes I had seen during the midnight shifts with the woman on the roof and the woman who came from Africa for an exorcism. There was one difference. When this man was staring at Chris, he sounded as if the straining of the voice increased. He looked with just intense evil in his eyes, it felt as if it were inhuman. He became visibly angrier as Chris approached him. Chris then backed up and broke the stare.

As the group stood over to the side, they tried to make sense of what they were witnessing. The consensus was that he was having a seizure. Chris, hearing this, walked up to Jason and took him to the side.

"Jason" he said, "I have seen hundreds of seizures as a medic in New York City, this was no seizure. In fact, I think he's possessed."

Jason looked back at Chris as if not expecting to hear that this could be a possibility at that moment. "Possessed? Wow ok." he replied.

Jason and Chris had developed a friendship over the short time they were together. They shared many stories and had a mutual respect for the accomplishments in work and ministry they had both been involved in. Jason believed as well in the reality of the devil and spiritual warfare but still didn't know what to make of this yet as it happened quite fast before their eyes. He understood one thing though, Chris believed what he saw.

The group formed a little circle as Jason began to pray for healing for whatever the man was experiencing. As they finished up at the market, the missionaries broke into little groups having their own little conversations. Chris walked among them on his own as he pondered what had happened today. Unlike the other two times at work, he could not let this one go.

As soon as they returned to the camp, Chris walked over to the Wi-Fi location created by the company. Chris and his family usually had a set time that he would check in daily. He placed a video call to Harmony to say goodnight as it was much later in New York.

As Harmony answered she could already see that he had something amazing to share. During the trip he had been sending pictures and sharing experiences back home with Harmony and the kids. They became excited for the calls each day as all this was foreign to their understanding of life.

After the kids finished saying goodnight, Chris began to share the events leading up to the man in the marketplace. When he told her that he believed this man was demonically possessed, she reacted surprised to herself but took it seriously. Chris had never really spoken of this type of activity much outside of a Biblical reading or a sermon in the Church. He had not shared the two events he witnessed at work with Harmony or thought much about this type of activity over the past few years.

Listening to him go over the events calmly and methodically, she soon realized that he must have had good reason to suspect this. She knew he was not one to get over dramatic or emotional but to look to rule everything else out first.

She agreed that it did not sound like a seizure either. She said, "No, a seizure wouldn't present that way. You're right."

Chris replied, "I'm telling you, I'm not sure what I just witnessed but it was not natural."

Later that evening, all the missionaries enjoyed a nice dinner together. The outdoor table was set next to the school overlooking the vast valley in the distance. It was always a welcome sight come evening as you could see other villages towards the bottom of the mountain. As they shared a meal, they began to share stories and lessons of the day's events as was the case every evening.

As talk of the future of the school and new ways to help bring in more children for education dominated the time, Chris was still stuck in the marketplace in his mind. When there was a break in the conversation he changed direction. He asked the group, "So what did you make of the guy on the ground in the market?"

One of them replied, "Yes that was crazy, the poor man was having a seizure and the villagers just watched."

Another person jumped in and explained, "They couldn't help. The way the law is set up here is that if a civilian begins the care for someone who is sick or hurt, and they go to the hospital, then the caregiver is responsible for the bills."

They were all very surprised but now it made sense. It was obvious no one wanted to get close to him.

Chris asked the group, "What if that was not the reason they stayed back?"

As they all sat around the picnic style table, a look of confusion could be seen on many of them.

"You're saying because they couldn't treat the seizure, they were afraid to help?" a woman asked.

Chris, seeing he had just been given an opportunity to explain, quickly responded. "No, I am saying that it was not a seizure. Not even close to one. Something else was happening to that man."

"What if they knew it and knew that something bad spiritually was happening?" Chris said.

The table began to closely listen, but he could tell by their faces, that they didn't believe it. Chris didn't care if they thought he was crazy. Jason looked over at Chris and by the look on his face could tell that he must have really experienced a life-changing event. Chris knew what he saw and was connecting the dots now. It was as if something had come alive inside of him. A chance meeting in a country, in a remote village on the other side of the world. From most people's point of view and using natural reasoning, it was a place he should never have been able to visit in his lifetime.

Two days later, Chris was on a plane back home, but he was not the same person as when he first arrived. He reflected over all the amazing new friendships and the experiences that would now be fixed in his memory for ever. As much as he was moved by everything that occurred and what he saw, one event kept replaying over and over in his mind. He kept asking himself a question, "What was happening to that man in the market?"

He was a man on a mission that was going to put the pieces together. What he was about to find would not only change his own life but his family's as well. God was now leading him to the final testing ground that would prepare him for his first battle in the spiritual realm.

CHAPTER THIRTEEN

A HAUNTED VACATION

Chris returned home to the States and began his search for the truth. He was committed to finding every piece of literature on the subject. Also, he was planning on bringing this up at his Church. He vowed to never speak of this again at Church after the embarrassing moment 9 years earlier, but now they were attending a different Church on eastern Long Island. Chris was now respected as a knowledgeable Christian and seasoned Evangelist, so he figured things might be better this time around. He needed to give it a try.

The Sunday following his arrival home, as the family was leaving service, Chris spotted one of the assistant pastors in the Church lobby. Chris and the pastor knew each other but didn't speak too often as he helped with the teens mostly. He was still a grown man with kids and Chris felt that being a pastor of a Church, he should be able to speak on this matter. After a few minutes of catching up and speaking about his adventure in Africa, Chris decided to bring up the subject.

"Let me ask you, do we have any deliverance ministries around here or anything like that?" Chris asked.

The pastor looked at him with a surprised look and smiled. Chris knew that look right away.

He thought to himself, "You gotta be kidding me. That damn look again."

The pastor responded laughing, "Deliverance? Why? are your kids possessed?"

Chris knew inside he wanted to lay him out flat on the floor. He looked at him with a half-smile, knowing he had made another mistake.

"Yeah, good one. Take it easy." Chris replied and walked out the door.

Ok, his Church, was obviously out of the question. As he researched the subject, he came upon deliverance ministries in the Evangelical Church. He observed a common theme that didn't make much sense to him Biblically. pastors were continually performing exorcisms on Church members or under a tent from those from those who were aware that they were possessed by demons. Two things the Bible never spoke about.

There was not much information on the subject regarding this type of work out in the streets from the Evangelical Church. Chris felt as if it was almost taboo to talk about it there and they just wanted to ignore the fact that it existed. He could not wrap his head around this since it was obviously very real, and people were suffering.

As he continued to search for help around demonic possessions outside the Church, he kept running into the same denomination, Catholicism. Those like him, who dealt with this phenomenon outside the Church, found their information here. Chris was amazed at the plethora of information that was offered on the subject.

A HAUNTED VACATION

He found studies going back centuries but not only that. The Catholic Exorcist seemed to have a methodical approach of how to deal with these events. They had a strong foundation and supported their findings with eyewitness accounts and even documented evidence. This was right up Chris's alley.

He then began to read and learn from laymen like him, but who had extensive experience in these types of cases occurring in homes and even on the streets. Unfortunately, some had passed away or were too difficult to reach. That was ok with Chris, as he knew he was still heading in the right direction.

While continuing his research, he learned of a religion called Santa Muerte, which was adapted by drug cartel members in Mexico. They would worship and make offerings to the Saint that represented the religion, for their drugs to make it over the border. Not only that, but to addict the user to keep the illegal drugs in high demand. Chris was blown away.

He did remember one thing from an Evangelical sermon once. The pastor was speaking on drug abuse. He said that drug abuse was a gateway or invitation for the devil to come into your life. The pastor was talking about it in more of a symbolic way at the time. Chris started to think now, but what if it can lead to possession?

During the week, he headed back to Times Square to reunite with his friends sleeping on the streets since returning from Africa. The sounds of "Hey Chris!" or "Where have you been?" could be heard around his area that he operated on over the past couple of years. He began to wonder about the many homeless people that he had encountered out here. Most of them were addicted to one drug or another.

"Was there something else behind the eyes, that was pulling the strings?" Chris thought.

He began to look at this ministry differently now as he would look for signs of demonic influence. The old saying, "The eyes are the windows to the soul" would be his starting point.

He would keep a keen observation on any eye abnormalities when God was brought into a conversation. He noticed on more than one occasion instead of resistance to the subject, the person was almost too happy to agree. It seemed odd to Chris, and he felt they were looking for a way to move on from the subject. Things were getting very strange out in the streets of New York City.

As the months went by, Chris seemed to slow down in this area. He felt he had a good understanding of this world, but he began to have reservations. He understood how dangerous it was after hearing story after story of activities occurring in the lives of those who become involved.

Chris was not one to jump into anything without being fully equipped but more than that, without being called to do something. He realized he was basically in new territory that even his Church couldn't help with and had to think hard on this. He was still trying to decide if this was a dangerous curiosity or somewhere God was leading him. It was something he conveyed many times to Pastor Tom over the months. Listening to his advice, he decided to take a break.

A HAUNTED VACATION

He changed his direction to family now as Harmony was finishing up the plans for a Sweet 16 vacation for Samantha. They had decided to head to a beautiful resort in Orlando. She was going to bring a few friends as they celebrated together. Sarah, Beckie, and Jake were going to stay behind for work and to care for the pets in the home.

It was the night before the trip. The truck was packed and the girls all sleeping over could be heard in the next room as the excitement was building for tomorrow's vacation to begin. They had no interest in sleeping as this would be a two-day trip.

In the next room, Chris was sound asleep as he had a long drive ahead of him. But something else was happening to Chris as he rested. If you looked at him from the outside, you would see a man getting a peaceful sleep. Inside his head was a horror film in the making.

As he dreamt, he found himself walking in the complete darkness of his hallway. With each step, his vision increased as his eyes slowly adapted to the darkness. As he approached the area where his den should be, he found himself in a strange room.

The room had the standard furniture and set up that you find in a nice hotel room. The room was lit up with a long, standing lamp in the corner of the room. Chris kept walking as if nothing was not how it should be. He was in a dream state and had no idea what reality was or not. Just as he took his first step into the hotel room area, he was lifted about five feet off the ground.

Caught totally by surprise, he was thrown into the wall and fell hard to the ground. Chris jumped to his feet and turned around in a state of panic but there was no one in the room with him.

Slam! Chris was lifted and smashed high into the corner of the ceiling this time before he could see it coming. He knew right away that he was dealing with a demon. He had that instinct or feeling you have in dreams where for whatever reason, the mind knows exactly what was happening at the time as unreal as it may be.

Chris began to call out in a loud voice, "In the name of Jesus Christ, I command you to leave!"

The invisible threat began to toss Chris back and forth with brutality as he was thrown literally around the room. Furniture was knocked over and on its sides as the impact from Chris's body was no match for it. Chris, attempting to regain his breath, found the strength for another command. He was met once again by a barrage of violence from the demon.

As he crawled over to a chair, he pulled himself up slowly. Battered and beaten, he was stunned as he could not figure out why this was happening. He kept hearing over and over in his head, "You have no faith; you have no faith."

He began to believe that he was no match for this demon. That he didn't know what he was doing and that he absolutely could not defeat it. Chris had this feeling like he was all alone in this room with a murderous demon and without any power whatsoever.

As he tried to catch his breath, the hotel door slammed open. In marched dozens of people, two by two. They were led by one man in a long red robe with a hood covering is head. He carried a long wooden staff with an upside down cross fixed to it. Chris could hear music filling the room. It sounded like music you would hear from a marching band as they made their way down the block during a parade. It was almost like they were celebrating.

As fast as they entered the room with thunderous marching, the room went silent and still. As everyone in the ranks turned to stare at Chris. Two men ran over quickly and tied him to the chair by his arms.

The man in the red robe approached him slowly as he lowered his hood. He was a tall, white man, with a gray beard and gray hair falling towards the back of his neck. He walked up to Chris displaying a very gentle face as Chris sat in the chair trying to recuperate. But it was not the kindness that you sense as genuine. There was a fakeness to it that was foreshadowing something bad in Chris's mind.

With an eerie, caring demeanor, the man asked, "Are you alright?"

Chris, still hyperventilating from the beating he just received by the demon, just stared at him. The man touched his arm as if to console him. Just then, the man slowly lifted his leg and smashed down with extreme force onto Chris's right foot. Chris's face turned red with anguish as the audible sounds of his bones cracking could be heard across the room.

The man, now with his revealed intent, ripped Chris's chain off his neck. As the man held it in his hand dangling, Chris noticed something odd. The chain he wore had two metal crosses on it instead of just one. The man reared his arm back and began to whip Chris on the top of his right forearm with the chain. Three strikes to his arm, left three long bloody lines.

"You don't deserve these!" The man shouted as he lifted them up to the cheering crowd.

As the man in the red hood disappeared into the crowd, a party type celebration once again took over the room. Chris sat there in defeat, but it wasn't over. A young attractive woman and what looked like her daughter knelt next to the broken Christian.

The little girl looked as if she could have been six or seven. She looked at her mother as she then looked back towards Chris with a strange smile. Chris had no idea what to expect.

This cute little girl looking up at Chris, said with a devious giggle, "The last one who attempted to get involved in this... he's not with us anymore... neither is his family."

As she laughed, her mother laughing with her, told her to stop it.

The little girl said in a playful manner, "Oops."

Chris's mind flooded with dread as he thought of the threat to his family. It was as if he could not control the thoughts in this dream. He began to cry uncontrollably. That awful, life-ending cry that most people have experienced one time or another in a dream as it combines with the most heart-breaking thoughts imagined.

Chris opened his eyes to the outside light of his neighbor's light in his face, as the dream state slowly materialized to reality. He did not wake in panic or sweating as you see in movies. He slowly sat up relieved that it was just a dream.

He waited for the sun to come up as he drank his coffee in the silence of the kitchen. He tried to make sense of the dream. He recalled every detail and could still feel the intensity of the confrontation with the demon and the man. He was worried he was being warned and that it was some coincidence that they were heading to a hotel in two days. But of course, it was just only a dream, right?

Still with questions, he decided to text Pastor Tom what had happened. Chris knew pastor was an early riser like him. Chris always enjoyed waking up to the daily morning scripture the pastor would send out to the men.

The following is a transcript of the text messages between the two:

Friday, July 26, 2019, 4:52 a.m.

Chris: Pray for me.

Pastor Tom: What happened?

Chris: Terrible dream last night. I was attacked and thrown around by a demon. As I was casting him away in Jesus's name, his followers came into the room with an upside down cross on a staff pole. They tied me to a chair, ripped off my cross and whipped me with it. They broke my right foot. A little girl told me that they were going to kill me. I remember in the dream; I was crying because I didn't want to tell my wife to get her involved.

A HAUNTED VACATION

Chris: Very real. I think it scared me straight.

Pastor Tom: Spiritual warfare is real. That's why none of us can give the devil a foothold.

As Harmony woke up, she headed to the kitchen like a queen with a good night's sleep and without a care in the world, "Where's my coffee?" she joked.

Chris decided he had to tell her about this strange dream. As he told her, she continued to listen while making her coffee. She always insisted she could multitask while listening to him speak. Something that bugged Chris, knowing that she always missed parts of his stories. He started to believe she had the unlisted medical illness called selective hearing.

As he finished telling the accounts of the dream, he looked for a response. Harmony finished stirring her cup and looked at Chris as she continued to the table. She said, "I guess you better bring holy water."

As funny as that moment seemed, Chris thought, "Hey why not?" and made sure to toss it in his suitcase before they left.

A couple of hours later, Chris, Harmony, Sam and her three friends drove off to her Sweet 16 celebration. They arrived in Orlando, Florida on Sunday afternoon as they made a few stops along the way to see some sites. They headed up the long driveway to the resort on a hill as the excitement could be heard from the girls in the back of the SUV.

A HAUNTED VACATION

The six of them marveled at the sight of the lobby. As they continued in, the see-through glass elevators could be seen filled with guests going up and down the 18 floor resort. The white tiled floor led to running ponds and comfortable sitting areas all around the wide opened lobby. It was all topped off with the feel of excited energy given off by parents and children as they were all here for the same purpose. To enjoy a great family vacation.

After a long drive from Long Island and finally making it to the resort with four teenage girls playing their music and yapping away for two days, Chris hit the sack. The girls went in for the night as well to the room next door. They had adjoining rooms on the seventh floor with balconies overlooking the inside of the resort. Chris could not wait to get some rest.

Harmony tapped Chris on the shoulder. "You didn't bless the rooms. You said you were going to when we got here."

She remembered as well how Chris would share new information he had been learning with her. He learned how important it was to bless the rooms you occupy when traveling. The reason behind it was not knowing who stayed there before you. What beliefs they had, lifestyles they led or energy they would leave behind.

Chris began to moan to leave him alone and pulled the covers higher. He said, "I'll do it tomorrow, look at this place, Its beautiful. I'm sure it's fine."

As Chris was asleep during the night, he heard a loud voice in his ear. A woman's voice. Startled as it was directly in his ear, he shot up. He looked over and saw Harmony sleeping. The voice was not a smooth sounding

A HAUNTED VACATION

pronunciation, but a hard broken word... sounding not as if an echo fading out but gaining intensity and volume.

Chris could not make out the word but didn't think much of it. He figured it was because he was exhausted and most likely from a dream. He put his head back down and drifted off. No more than a few moments later, the same sound in his ear again. This time he heard it more clearly.

He jumped up again and looked around the room. He still couldn't make out the entire word, but it had a hard sounding G at the beginning. Chris had enough at this point. This was strange enough that he believed something was going on and was not taking any chances now.

He stepped completely out of the bed, as he spoke aloud "Oh hell no."

He went over to the suitcase, pulled out the holy water and began to pray for intercession from God. He walked from one end of the room to the other. As he walked by Harmony, he shook his head, envious of her clear head. He smiled as he doused her with water as well.

The rest of the night was uneventful... in their room at least.

Over in the girl's room, they were doing what teenage girls do. Eating snacks, playing on their phones, and watching horror movies. Kim put on a scary movie about shadow people as they all had a good time laughing and screaming during the film. As far as the girls knew, that was all that happened that night.

Monday morning everyone met in the hallway outside the rooms around 7:30 a.m. for breakfast.

Samantha, who was making a Vlog, or video album for her birthday, began to speak to the camera on the phone, as they all headed down the hall. Suddenly Chris heard something shocking from one of the girls as she spoke to Harmony.

"There is a huge handprint on our wall."

Before Chris could react, Samantha spoke up as she was still filming. "I told my mom already," she said.

Chris raised both hands as a person who was left out of the loop. He looked at Harmony. "Really? That might be something for me to know?"

Meanwhile Samantha knew what dad had been experiencing and learning about over the last year. She never took anything too seriously, so it didn't surprise him much when she didn't tell him. They all probably got a laugh out of it. Not Chris though. Hearing this, he told the group to keep heading to the kitchen and he would meet them there. He was going to see what was on the wall.

As he entered the room, he walked by the bathroom on the left, which had a smoked glass sliding door. As he continued, a long mirror was on the wall to the right. One step further and there was the print. Between the TV and the mirror was a very large type of handprint close to six feet off the ground.

As Chris took a closer look he could see abnormalities in the print. The fingers were larger and not the same length as human fingers if someone leaned on the wall. Also, it looked as if there were only four fingers instead of five. Chris took out his phone and snapped a couple of pictures from different angles.

As strange as this was, Chris was not interested in thinking any more about this. He wanted to rationalize it away as he began to put logical reasons how this could have happened in the natural. This was to be a family vacation. He closed the door and headed to breakfast.

Before leaving the hotel, the maid knocked at the door. She handed Harmony fresh water bottles and towels for both rooms. Harmony let her know that it was ok for her to put the items for the girls in their room. The maid was nonverbal and could not communicate in words. She gave a nod and a smile but still left all the items with Harmony.

After a fun day sightseeing and enjoying the Florida sun, the parents and girls split up for the night. As the nightly thunderstorm was heading in, Chris and Harmony took in a movie in their room while the girls headed out to the pool for a swim. The storms were predictable as they came in every night around eight or nine but didn't last long.

After about a half hour the pool closed because of the weather and the girls returned to the room. As the girls walked just past the mirror, they all made a comment about a strange smell in the room. It was strong enough that each one who passed it made a face. It was a foreign smell to them.

The girls went on with their night, making the best of it in the room. Later that night, they all drifted off to sleep. All the lights were off. With the shades drawn as well, the room would remain dark even when the sun rose. The only light in the room that remained was the dimly lit bathroom hidden behind the smoked glass of the sliding door.

Then, bang, bang, bang could be heard in the room. Bang, bang, bang once again. Michala woke up. She and Kim were sleeping in the bed closest to the balcony. She heard the noise and wondered what it could be. She looked toward the lit area by the bathroom. As she looked through the reflection of the wall mounted mirror, she could see directly into the bathroom.

On the other side of the glass door, she could see a dark figure. It looked as if the door was stuck, and a person was trying to open it to get out of the bathroom. Logically, she immediately thought it was one of the girls stuck and began to take her first step off the bed to help. Suddenly she saw something that froze her in her tracks. She looked to her right across the entire room and could see that all the girls were still sleeping in their beds.

If the girls are sleeping, "Who was in the bathroom?" she thought. Michala began to shake Kim.

"Kim, wake up! Wake up!" she whispered.

Kim opened her eyes slowly. "What, what's going on?" she asked.

Michala in a panic said, "Someone's in the bathroom!" as she pointed continuously towards the bathroom.

Kim sat up quickly; she looked through the mirror as well and saw the figure.

Suddenly, Bang! The door slammed shut and the bathroom light went off. Both Michala and Kim started screaming as Samantha woke up from all their commotion.

Samantha said confused, "Why are you guys screaming?"

As the two girls explained what had happened, Samantha didn't buy it. She told them it was probably her mother in the bathroom. As Samantha got out of bed to make her way to the bathroom, Michala begged her not to go. Samantha, having second thoughts, grabbed her phone and decided to text her mom from her bed.

Harmony replied moments later that it was not her, but she was about to come over and bring bottled water. It was actually 6:30 in the morning. Samantha told her what happened as Harmony now rushed over. Harmony walked right into the dark bathroom. She noticed right away that the light switch was still in the up position even though the light was off.

Harmony walked over to Michala and Kim. She noticed that Michala was pale and believed she had experienced something. The girls were shaken. Harmony knew only one thing to do in that situation. She prayed with the girls. Although no one knew what had just occurred in that room, Harmony fell back to her faith and went to the Lord for help.

When they finished praying, Harmony called Chris. Chris had left earlier for a run around the resort. The resort had a clay road for joggers to give them an opportunity to see the whole complex. It was a very peaceful way to start a day as there were only a few people jogging at this time and everyone was spread well apart.

A HAUNTED VACATION

When Harmony reached him, he had just walked back inside the building. As Harmony told him what had happened, he was shocked. That was the last thing anyone would probably expect to hear. Chris told her he would be right up and went to hang up but then stopped.

"Wait!" he shouted. "Do you know what time this happened exactly?" he asked.

Harmony could be heard asking the girls.

She replied, "Probably 15 minutes ago. Why?"

Chris responded, "Ahh, no big reason, just wondering. I'll be right there."

Chris hung up the phone, stepped back outside and looked towards the lake area on the grounds. He started to recollect, but "it couldn't be," he thought.

He started to go over the last 15 minutes in his mind. He was having a nice early morning run but then he remembered why he stopped the run. As he approached the lake area, there was a mist covering an area where trees and grass made its home on the edge of the water.

When he began to run closer to that area he was overcome with panic. He remembered the kid who worked there telling him yesterday, to beware of gators. The park keeps an eye out, but one or two each year slip in.

Unlike on yesterday's run, the feeling this morning was so overwhelming as he approached that area, it was as if something was telling him that he was about to be ambushed. It was the perfectly secluded part of the track,

and no one would know. Chris stopped and sprinted back to the building. Until the phone call, he just figured it was his stupid nerves, but now with the combination of events over the last two days, he didn't discount anything.
The first thing Chris did when he got to the room was to interview the girls. Sam had now prepared them and let them know her dad kind of has some experience with this stuff. The girls were obviously surprised.

    Chris first spoke to Michala as he could see that she was still in a little shock. She was the daughter of an NYPD detective he knew, and she was a good kid. He would have been very surprised if she made it up. After listening to the story and the other girls, Chris was convinced they were telling the truth and saw something profound.

    Not sure what to do yet, they took the family out for the day as they went to visit surrounding theme parks. Chris knew he couldn't say anything to the desk about this yet because he knew from experience, that never went over well. Besides, if they switched rooms, someone else could possibly be at risk. Also, they paid a fortune for this trip, he wasn't going anywhere.

    When they returned from a relaxing day out after the horror that occurred that morning, the plan was to go out for a nice dinner in the evening. When Chris and Harmony walked into their room, the room was all cleaned as the bed was made and tidied up. But they also noticed once again, the water and towels for the girls were left in their room. As Harmony went next door, the girl's room was not cleaned either. Harmony called down to the desk to finally complain but Chris was quietly taking notice and continually adding things up on the fly.

A HAUNTED VACATION

Later that night around 11:00 p.m., Chris was down in the outside lounge area smoking a cigar. Harmony was off to bed as with her Lupus she tired easily. Chris needed to relax and figure out what to do tonight about the girl's room. The girls were going to go for a night swim, so he had just a little longer to decide.

He gave Pastor Tom a quick call to update him. He was very concerned about the events taking place. The two men prayed on the phone as Chris searched for discernment of how to proceed.

The girls on the way to the pool spotted Chris. They all ran over with towels in hand as he could hear them approaching. They sat down around him, telling him that they were not sleeping in that room tonight. They were laughing and joking but Chris knew they were serious.

"We're all going to sleep on your floor tonight," Kim chuckled.

Then Michala put her parents on facetime, as all the girls were calling home and friends. The girls couldn't wait to tell them. The parents joked as most people don't take this stuff too seriously. They probably figured the girls were horsing around or that he was scaring them. Chris was always known as a prankster.

As the girls left for the pool, Chris now realized that this was becoming a public spectacle. He laughed to himself as he remembered having a conversation with Michala's dad at one of the girls' soccer games before they left. Both men being cops in the department, had a respect and trust for each other knowing their kids were always in good hands. The last thing Chris remembered saying to him was, "Don't worry I'll look after her."

Now he brought his daughter to a high-end resort in one of the most famous attraction areas in the country, and she's being terrorized by an evil spirit. "Good job Chris," he spoke out loud as if he was lost in his thoughts.

Suddenly he became angry as a parent would when someone threatens their child. This was not just some little thing. Something was targeting his children. The children who were under his care. Now it was personal. It was now clear there was only one thing to do since there was no one to call. Take care of this thing himself.

He sent Samantha a text message to stay away from the room and he would let her know when to come back. Samantha knew what that meant and told the girls as they huddled around with playful curiosity.

Chris stood up and headed to the girl's room. First, he popped into his room to grab the holy water from his bag and picked up a special book he would need. Harmony seemed to be sleeping through all the drama this entire trip, which at least brought a smile to his face that he desperately needed for that moment. He grabbed the key to the girl's room and swiped the door.

As Chris entered, he could see that the lamp at the other end of the room was on. Just then something clicked...the dream, a hotel room, a demon, a warning? Chris felt a rush of fear come over him as he couldn't believe it. Looking straight ahead, he bolted for the balcony. He opened the sliding glass door and stepped outside like someone looking for air after being underwater too long.

A HAUNTED VACATION

Chris stood on the seventh-floor balcony in a black tightly fitted athletic shirt, gray gym shorts and sneakers. Hardly the attire you would expect to see by those performing this type of ritual blessing.

As he leaned outward on the balcony railing, he took in the moment overlooking the beautiful resort. It was truly an amazing sight to see at night as the array of colorful lights lit up the midnight sky. He could see his daughter, Samantha, and her three friends horsing around in the pool. The soothing sound of the waterfall emptying into the pool filled the air. In the distance, he could see a hot air balloon rising with guests at the world-famous family amusement park across the way. This was to be the place families come to hide from the rat race of life or even for just a break from those stressful daily responsibilities.

For months, he looked forward to this trip as much as the kids. Traveling to busy New York City for close to 25 years for work was more than enough reason for anyone to desire such a vacation, not to mention a cop. But this relaxing getaway was not to be for Chris. After the events of the past two days at the resort, he quickly realized that he was here for a different purpose.

This was not something he signed up for or something he even wanted to do, but here he was. A fork in the road, a blue pill or red pill moment of life was presented before his eyes, and he would have a major decision to make. A decision that would have a much greater impact than the temporal issues in their own little lives but a decision that could reap systemic results in whichever direction he chose.

Chris unknowingly was not called here for a vacation but for battle. This was personal. An attack on his family was considered a declaration of war. There was no turning back now. Faith, knowledge, and courage would be his weapons of war in this new world that he was about to enter. A world where size and stature are insignificant, but only faith in the one true God matters. This battle was not against flesh and blood but the kingdom of darkness, the devil himself. Chris was now taking part in this raging war that has been going on between God, the devil, and occurring through the duality of worlds since creation.

He took a deep breath and slowly turned around leaving the serenity of the heavenly view. As he slowly stepped forward towards the sliding glass door, he removed the book from under his arm. It was his Bible. His own strategic playbook, which can be compared to what a coach would use in a big game. Only this was no game. Here the stakes were much greater. This could possibly be a matter of life and death.

He thought to himself, "Am I really doing this?"

He focused once more on the dream just days before with a strict warning to stay away from this specific ministry. Ignoring the warning and remembering the caution from his pastor back home, he pushed forward to his destiny. He opened the sliding door into his daughter's hotel room with caution. The sounds of the resort that once filled his ears, were now drowned out by the silence of the room. The silence soon gave way to the rapid beating of his pounding heart.

He did not know what to expect. Sure, he read about this kind of thing in books and watched movies on it, but this was different. This was happening in real time, and he was not an actor in a movie. He paused for a moment, overcome once again with fear.

He began to question himself, "Who am I to do this? I don't belong here."

He continued, "In fact, I don't even want to be here."

He desperately wanted to be that husband and dad, like all the others enjoying this trip with their families. He knew that all he had to do was turn around towards the balcony view once more and that could be his life again. It was as if doubt was drawing him back once again to what he once thought as "reality." Suddenly as fast as the doubt came upon him, came an inner strength he could not explain.

He regained his composure realizing that God was his strength and would never leave him nor forsake him in this moment, just as He had shown Chris many times before. With each step forward, it was as if a piece of invisible armor were attaching itself to various parts of his body. Faith was his armor, knowledge was his sword and the call of God, was his authority.

As he took his first step into the room, it became clear that this moment was no accident. He was not some random guy in the wrong place at the wrong time. No, he was being prepared for this one moment, his entire life.

Chris began the ritual blessing. He began to read scripture as he blessed the room with holy water. He knew he would have to rely more on his memory of scripture as he was alone. It would not be a good tactical move to drop his head and not always see the surrounding area. He knew he had to call this demon out in the authority of Jesus, but he remembered how bad that went in the dream.

A HAUNTED VACATION

As Chris proceeded and prepared for anything, he was surprised at what he found. Nothing. Nothing was happening, in fact the room was silent. As Chris finished the prayer, he realized the room felt much better. He felt unafraid and had no issues even walking into the bathroom. It was a feeling that was not there before the blessing.

There was no fight, no battle. He expected the worst, but it was if the spirit left without a fight. Still, Chris was not disappointed by the anticlimactic battle. He called the girls back to the room. The girls felt the exact same way about the room as Chris and decided to stay in the room for the night.

For the next three nights, the trip went without a hitch. The girls did not have any other activity in the room, and everything went well. A few days later, the family packed up and left. Just like that it was over.

Unlike everyone else, Chris was glad to head home. Chris and Harmony looked to the back of the truck to watch the girls laughing as they took selfies and pics of each other. They were relieved that the girls still had a good time. As they drove home, Chris was looking forward to putting this whole event behind him. But little did he know the girls were making videos on social media and telling their parents what Chris had done in the room.

Chris was enjoying himself when Samantha yelled out to her dad.

"Hey Dad, Michala's dad, just sent her a funny text." she said.

Chris responded, "Oh yeah? What was it?"

A HAUNTED VACATION

She read it from Michala's phone. "I didn't know Sam's dad is a ghostbuster?"

Chris looked at Harmony as he dropped his head in embarrassment. He knew what was coming when he got home and suddenly, he was not in such a rush. This was not going to be the end by any means... it was only the beginning.

A HAUNTED VACATION

CHAPTER FOURTEEN

LEAVING FLORIDA

A week went by since the return home from Florida and between work and busy family life, the past vacation had to take a back seat. Chris somehow felt that he missed that part about a relaxing getaway. It seemed that during the Florida trip, he was involved in more investigation work than he had at the precinct in recent years.

He was now called "The Broom" by most cops since all his duties revolved around making sure the precinct building was running on all cylinders. He basically had more responsibility now and had to report to more NYPD brass than before, but working the streets was not one of them. A couple of the younger cops would call him Dad as Chris was nearing 50 and the same age as their parents. He was also in charge of equipment, lockers, and other things the cops would need.

Chris liked to say, "Just think of me like Red Redding from the movie Shawshank Redemption. I'll get you whatever you need."

After the blessing of the room and the unexpected ordinary events that took place during it, Chris felt it was over. Now it was time to switch his attention back to "real" life on Long Island.

It was now a Saturday, almost a week since returning from the trip. Chris was on the back deck enjoying the nice weather. He was looking through photos of the trip. He smiled as he saw goofy family pics around the resort as well as the parks they visited. On the outside, it sure looked as if it was the typical family vacation.

As he continued to scroll, he came across a strange photo in the mix. It stood out right away as a picture that must have been taken by accident. Many times, Chris would look down and his phone was in camera mode as he must have clicked a button by accident this time as well. He looked with surprise at what was in the picture.

As he looked closely, he could see that from the angle, it was the girl's room. He could see the wall mirror and part of his reflection as well. They were the same clothes as he wore when he was blessing the room. But what was in front of the mirror confused him.

There looked to be a black shadow. It was a misty figure with a definite outline, and it was right next to him in that room. Chris zoomed in on the area and looked from all different angles. There was no flash, no light reflection or anything else. There was no denying it, this was something he couldn't explain.

Chris opened the info regarding the photo to try and get an idea when it was taken. He could see that at its position in the roll, it was the night of the blessing, but when? As he found the time stamp, he saw 11:47 p.m. Chris looked up for a moment trying to recall the timeline of events. Suddenly he felt a sick feeling come over him as he realized that picture was taken after the blessing was completed. He was looking around the room before the girls returned. It was still there!

LEAVING FLORIDA

He discussed his findings with Harmony and after thinking long and hard on this, they both agreed Chris should contact the hotel. Chris felt that there could be another family in trouble and didn't feel right, just turning his back. But he had another problem. How does he call the hotel and tell them they have an evil spirit running around one of their rooms without sounding like a nut? He figured there was probably no way to, so he began to reach out.

He decided to first send a nice email about what a beautiful hotel they have and to thank them for a great family vacation. He chuckled under his breath as he typed that line, "yeah, family vacation."

He then mentioned he did have one matter to discuss that was important regarding their stay. Chris received a return email later that day. He was impressed with their promptness as he was ready to drop the bomb on them.

As Chris began his reply to the hotel, he mentioned the events of their stay as he attempted to ease it in. With this began the game of "We do not handle these types of complaints; I will send you to the right department," type of emails in response.

It became a frustrating game as Chris would be sent from one department to the next and asking for his pedigree information all over again. Chris became impatient as he knew what they were doing. Finally, he had enough and blasted the hotel for how they were handling this complaint. Chris listed all the different departments he communicated with, time stamps of emails and more. By the end of the week, Chris received an email from the Director of Operations himself. They scheduled a phone call.

LEAVING FLORIDA

As Chris waited for the scheduled call next week, He and his wife, took a nice day trip to the east end of Long Island that weekend. It was a beautiful little town made up of independently owned shops that counted on the summer tourists for their living. It was always a nice place to come as it was close to the ocean. Just like family vacation spots, it gave off that peaceful atmosphere where you can let go of that daily stress, even if it was for one day.

As they walked up and down the smooth sidewalks, looking in the shops, Chris noticed an interesting looking bookstore. Harmony was just walking into a little shop with pocketbooks, so Chris told her he would be right back.

As Chris walked in, he noticed right away that it was more than a bookstore. As well as books, the shelves were filled with crystals, healing charms and many other items of that type. He knew immediately what type of place he was in. He decided to look at the books to see if he could find some information on the spirit he captured in the photo.

As he was going through the books, the woman behind the counter approached and asked if he needed any help. She was very friendly and noticed the types of books he was looking through in the Spirituality section. Chris explained some pertinent details of what and why he was looking at the books. He could see right away that this was not the first time she had heard something like this. She asked if she could see the photo. She explained that she had helped paranormal investigators solve some cases in the past by looking at photos.

Chris was more than happy to get another opinion and especially someone who could give real insight. He handed her the phone. Her reaction was a little more than he was looking for.

She handed him back the phone in a rush and said, "You definitely have something bad there. Oh yes!" She walked back to the counter. Chris followed her to try to get some more insight.

"Bad? How bad are we talking here?" he asked.

She replied, "That is a dark spirit, a malevolent spirit."

Chris could tell this was not something she wanted to speak about anymore. He offered his hand out and thanked her. As they shook hands, her face turned from a smile to scared. She turned and walked away and began to place a phone call. Chris walked out as he sensed something as well.

He knew after being in the store and talking to the woman that she was some sort of psychic or possibly involved in witchcraft. Chris had never told her of his Christian faith and beliefs. When they made physical contact, he believed she felt something she possibly did not appreciate, a Christian.

Chris began a much deeper look into the hotel. As he researched, he was amazed to find that there were child deaths at this location. One child drowned in the pool while another fell off the balcony to his death. What was even more interesting was that the boy who fell off the balcony had the anniversary of his death at the same time the DeFlorio's visited the resort.

Chris had one other question that needed to be answered. What was the room that this occurred in? As he read through the articles, he could find no mention of the room or even the floor. He printed out all the material, compiled the case file and waited for the call. He would look for clarity when he spoke to the Director.

A couple of days later, Chris was at work at the 32 Precinct. He had a scheduled call with the Director of Operations from the hotel at 2:00 p.m. It wouldn't be an issue for Chris since he knew all the areas in the four-story building where he could find privacy. Chris set up in a downstairs office he used as his own. The outside of the door read, "Custodial Closet," which left the office hidden to most of the cops and supervisors.

The phone rang promptly at 2:00 p.m. Chris and the Director exchanged pleasantries as Chris began to explain the event. He told him about the step-by-step occurrences and how he handled it. Chris also advised him to interview the custodial staff, since one of the workers had an obvious aversion to the room.

To Chris's surprise, the Director explained that they had already interviewed them as they had begun their own look into this claim. Chris was glad to see that he was taking this seriously enough to speak to them. The two men were having a very good exchange as the Director also realized that Chris was an NYPD Cop, which gave much more credibility now. It didn't hurt that the Director was a believer in the supernatural too.

Chris went on to explain that he did his own background check on the hotel. Chris said, "I did some looking into the hotel. I am not sure if you are aware but there have been multiple children's deaths over the years at this resort."

Chris knew where he wanted to throw this into the conversation to hear his first reaction. This would give true insight into how much the hotel knew, and it proved to be an effective method.

The Director responded after a pause, "Oh, you know about that?"

Chris was actually surprised that he knew as well. Chris was expecting more of a surprise with the new information but that was not what happened.

Chris continued, "Listen, I am not looking for a free vacation here. I'm telling you that if this is not handled, you may have a much bigger problem in the future."

The Director was very receptive and asked Chris to email over the photos of the handprint on the wall, the spirit he captured in the picture and anything else he had. He told Chris that they would investigate this situation some more and get back to him during the week.

Chris walked into the locker room after the call. He ran into Andrew, a fellow Officer. They began to catch up on what's been going on with each other. Chris, fresh off the phone call, decided to bring up the subject of the paranormal to get a feel if he would be receptive or one of the scoffers. To his relief, Andrew was a big believer in the subject and even spoke of his personal stories.

As Chris told him what had happened to his family. Andrew gave Chris a strange look. Chris stopped to inquire what he was thinking.

Andrew asked surprised, "Wait! That was you?"

Now Chris was very confused. He replied, "What was me?"

Andrew said I saw this story on TikTok the other day. A young girl told the same story. It was creepy."

Chris asked him to show him the video. Chris figured it was a similar story but was curious anyway. After a few minutes, Andrew showed him what he saw. Chris looked at it and was shocked. It was Michala.

He shouted, "That's my daughter's friend, one of the girls with us, you've got to be kidding me!"

Andrew responded laughing, "Bro, look at this number, this video is viral."

Chris sat there shaking his head. He decided to show Andrew the photo of the spirit from the room. He figured he knows a lot about the event now anyway and has some experience understanding this stuff, why not?

As Andrew looked at the picture, he began to trace his finger around the black mist.

He said confidently, "That looks like a kid."

"A kid?" Chris quickly replied.

Andrew showed him the specific features as he described what he saw. Chris agreed. Also, he knew that Andrew had no idea of the prior deaths of the children, so this made it more compelling. Chris couldn't believe the twists and turns of what had unfolded since their fateful trip

LEAVING FLORIDA

to Florida. This story was getting bigger with each conversation.

Over the week, Chris decided he was going to create a formal case file on this event. He was going to set up some formal interviews on recording of everyone involved. Over the next several days, Chris interviewed Samantha, the girls and even Harmony on recording to document what had happened in perfect detail. After seeing how this one event was revealing more information daily, this was the next logical move to preserve it.

A couple of days later, Chris was having his morning coffee before he headed to work. It was 4 am and one of his favorite times of the day as most of the world was still asleep and seemed at peace, if not only for a few more minutes. He was sitting on the couch as their little dog Chevy, slept on the other end.

Suddenly, Chris could hear what sounded like squeaks on the wood floor as if someone were taking slow steps in his direction. He looked up but no one was there. The cracking of the wood floor moved closer and closer to where Chris was sitting but again, he saw no one.

Just then, Chevy jumped to his feet on the cushion as he attempted to balance himself. He stared with laser focus at the invisible footsteps and began to growl ferociously. Chris looked with shock as he could see the fangs of Chevy's teeth as he continued to growl. Chevy ran over to Chris and dropped in his lap.

Chris pulled out his cross and began to pray unceasingly to Jesus for protection. The footsteps stopped and Chevy seemed to go back to normal. From that day forward, Chevy became one of his greatest warning systems in the home for paranormal activity.

Chris stood up. He walked into the kitchen, put his coffee mug in the sink and said, "This is going to be one hell of a day."

One week later Chris received an email from the Director of the hotel. After a quick reflection on the bad results in the past whenever he spoke on this topic, Chris was not expecting anything different.

Chris sat down and prepared himself before he clicked to open the entire email. What was he going to read? Was this going to be added to the lists of embarrassments over the years? He clicked on the link and began to read. After he finished reading, he walked out onto his deck looking across the yard. He just stared.

The email read, "Based on our investigation and your compelling evidence detailing the events, the room has been shut down to guests. It has been reassigned to inventory and will be used for overstock. Thank you for your help in bringing this situation to our attention."

Chris stood there feeling closure and a sense of accomplishment. He took the risk of going public with what happened and at the very least, he helped the situation. Thinking back from the first event all the way until today, he began to see things more clearly. His police and paramedic training, combined with his faith in God, made this work something he may be equipped to continue in.

Harmony walked outside as Chris recounted the events of the last few minutes. He told her about the calling he is feeling and the door he believes God is opening again. He said, "What if I can help someone else? Someone that is going through what we did and has no one to help? I need to do this."

By this time, Harmony was aware of the emails and information Chris was finding on the case since they returned from the trip. When she read the last email, she agreed. She obviously knew this was real and was ecstatic as well that he got the room shut down. Chris said, "Ok then, I'm doing this."

Chris began to walk back into the house. Just before he took his first step in, Harmony stopped him. "Just one thing," she said. "You're not doing it alone. I will never let you go through what you did that night at the hotel again."

Chris looked back with a smile as if thinking how to reply. Chris said, "Ok but you know what this means right?"

Harmony stared at Chris as she was waiting to hear something profound but that's not what she heard. He said, "You may miss out on some of that beauty sleep you love so much."

Harmony looked back with a smirk. "Very funny," she replied.

Chris and Harmony went on to work on many cases together. It seemed just as God had precisely ordained each step in preparation for them to enter this ministry, He continued the same work in bringing them through it. They grew in experience, processing and learning from each new case. As one case would end, another case with new adventures would find them.

Chris found himself helping many in the NYPD, ranging from police officers to supervisors themselves as word spread of his ministry. This seemed to be just the beginning as he was called in to help two officers who came under a spiritual attack in the precinct in 2020. The couple was now making a name as headlines were developing. But as far as Chris was concerned, there was one interaction with a cop that beat them all. An event that came out of Texas.

Chris watched firsthand, as his old partner, Rich, now a retired Detective, gave his life to the Lord. The same man that couldn't understand what happened to Chris in 2009, was now a changed person in God as well. His life became a living testimony and returned to the Church after witnessing Chris and Harmony in their new calling. People were now being saved as well.

All the while, their marriage was transformed in ways no one could understand as they worked in this ministry together. God had showed them in their marriage to trust themselves to the other. Now this was about to play out in ministry as they would only have each other under God. As the cases grew in intensity, God would continue the preparation for a larger battle to come.

Chris would be the watcher over his wife in the demonic infested homes they entered. Harmony kept her word as she would never let her husband perform a confrontational blessing again. What she didn't know at the time was how much she would have to hold that vow, as his life would depend on her in 2021 while visiting a little town in... Connecticut.

CHAPTER FIFTEEN

CONNECTICUT
The Confrontation

As Chris and Harmony were about to enter the attic, they attempted to mentally prepare in the best way they could. Over the span of just a few weeks, the case jumped from infestation of a home to attempting the possession of a four year-old boy. Here they were again, just the two of them. The outcasts from either side of the Church. Not qualified enough for one denomination but too crazy for another. None of that mattered on this Sunday morning as the safety of a family being terrorized by a demon was the only concern.

Chris and Harmony stepped back for a moment for some personal prayer with God. Harmony then fired up the charcoal in the brass censer and began to place droplets of frankincense on top. As the smoke began to slowly seep through air vents in the lid, she handed it to her husband. Chris slowly began his ascent climbing the ladder towards the dislodged attic cover. He couldn't help but think of how there were thousands of people at Church services right now, as they were walking into the greatest Spiritual warfare imaginable.

When Chris reached the top, he gave one hard shove of the cover as it shot clear off into the attic. He reached through the opening with just his hand and laid the smoking burner on the attic floor. He sat outside the attic, resting on the ladder steps as the room filled with Frankincense. Frankincense was an act of worship to the Lord in the Old Testament. Also, it was an affirmation to Jesus Christ as God in the flesh, as He received it as a gift from the Magi after His birth.

He likened it to a SWAT Officer throwing in a flash bang, to help gain access to an area held by a perpetrator. Chris found this was always a necessary part of the blessing as he was now manifesting the kingdom of God as he consecrated the attic to the Lord. He knew Marbas was not going to find this pleasant and hopefully put him on his heels for the moment. This would let him know they were not here for games and the battle was on.

Chris took book after book out and laid them out across the air conditioning duct as he prepared for the blessing. First, he would read specific Scriptures from his English translation followed by the scripture in the original Greek. After that he would begin the confrontational stage of the blessing going head-to-head with the mighty demon.

He understood from scripture how Jesus spoke of different types of demons, having different methods to exorcise them. Chris had a feeling he would have to run the gamut today against Marbas and who knows how many minions he brought with him.

As Chris finished up the English translations of Scripture, he began **Colossians 1:16 in the Greek.** *For by Him were all things created, that are in heaven, and that are in earth, visible and invisible, whether they be thrones, or dominions, or principalities, or powers: all things were created by Him, and for Him.*

CONNECTICUT – THE CONFRONTATION

Halfway through the scripture, the room became much darker as the sun was hidden under the incoming dark clouds. The attic began to take on a strange feeling as if they had just lost home field advantage.

Chris continued in the Greek **to John 1:1 *In the beginning was the Word, and the Word was with God, and the Word was God***, as the clouds seemed to unload a barrage of rain a top the roof.

They felt as if they were only separated from being swept away by a thin piece of plywood that could fall in on them at any moment. The only window that could access the outside world looked as if a car window was going through a car wash. Chris knew they were getting close to the confrontation as the entity was beginning to slowly let them know he was on his way.

Harmony broke her hands from prayer and picked up the large cross they used for the blessings. This was not just a means of protection but to signify to the enemy, **Christ crucified, and the victory was already won**.

As Chris read on, Harmony rotated her gaze around the room keeping an eye out for anything suspicious. She couldn't help but feel that something was creeping up from behind in the darkness of the attic.

Chris began to speak in incomplete sentences while reading.

Harmony asked, "What's wrong?"

Chris responded in some distress, "I smell something bad, it's horrible."

Harmony didn't smell anything yet from where she was standing. Chris began to exhale heavily as the smell was obviously interfering with his speech.

Moments later, Harmony began to yell over the attempted reading, "I smell it, I smell it."

"It smells like feces. Keep reading, keep reading."

Harmony ran to Chris as he began to get weak in the knees. She helped lift him and helped him over to the air vents to lean on.

Now the room began to heat up. This was not your typical activity they were used to where a room might become cold when an entity is attempting to manifest. The room became much warmer this time over the last minute or so. There is never a set textbook to follow when a battle is in motion as both sides can pull from their arsenal at any time and change direction.

Chris decided to break from reading as they would go to the LORDS PRAYER. Just as they were about to begin, Chris began to feel the shocks to the forearms. There it was. Something was entering his space. It was too early to confirm who they were dealing with, as many times, weaker demons in the hierarchy are sent in first to wear down the Christian.

In Unity the couple began the prayer,

"Our Father, who art in Heaven, Hallowed be Thy name."

Chris heard a strange sound. He threw his head up and quickly looked around the attic as Harmony continued in the prayer.

"Thy kingdom come; Thy will be done."

Chris became distracted as he heard the noise again. Harmony now heard it as her questionable eyes revealed.

"It sounded like a growl or something," Harmony said.

But Chris noticed something else. The strange noise was actually in sync with the prayer. Whatever was causing this sound was making another attempt to distract them from continuing the prayer. This was a common tactic of the Devil, as prayer to God was his Achilles heel.

As Harmony continued reciting the prayer, Chris scanned the room, focused, and determined to pinpoint the sound. He was being sucked in by his investigative curiosity. The Devil knows how to tempt each man according to his weaknesses. He found Chris's in that attic.

She reached the end of the prayer, ***"And lead us not into temptation, but deliver us from the evil one."***

The sound was now louder than ever but Chris picked it up this time. He looked at Harmony.

"Hold on," he said. "That wasn't a growl, that was a roar. Are you kidding me?"

He knew what he heard but was in disbelief. Chris knew Marbas had arrived and was manifesting right before their eyes.

CONNECTICUT – THE CONFRONTATION

The couple found themselves alone and out ***two by two*** (as he often quoted the Biblical text) so many times before that it was almost expected. They were no strangers to leaving comfort for the sake of Christ and love for their neighbors, no matter what the cost. This was who they became through ministry and always felt there was no higher calling than to live out the proclamation of the Gospel in their lives.

Now the stakes were much higher. The Connecticut family were not the only ones in danger anymore. Chris, Harmony and possibly their own children were now targets themselves. Years ago, Chris chose to ignore that strict warning from the dream to keep away from this ministry and now may have to live with the consequences. The battle was real, and they knew it was either time to dig in or retreat...So they dug in for the final battle.

One thing Chris was glad about was that at least this thing was away from Tommy since he was not at the location. Chris told Harmony to yell down to Glenda to inquire if she made any noise downstairs. It was of first importance to find a rational reason for the sound. This would be very refreshing to know that it was something Glenda might have done accidentally or really anything else besides a demon!

"What was that noise?" Harmony yelled down from the attic to the first-floor den.

Glenda's sister, Bo, quickly replied, "I thought it was you guys! It's nothing down here...It's up there with you."

They were both surprised to hear Bo's voice. What they didn't know was that Tommy had been dropped off at

CONNECTICUT – THE CONFRONTATION

the house during the blessing. They sat outside on the porch as they watched the rain come down. As Chris and Harmony were in that last battle, little Tommy was giving Glenda a play by play outside to what was happening in the attic.

When Tommy first sat down on the porch, he asked Glenda, "Who's here?"

Glenda replied, "Chris and Harmony are here."

Tommy said, "They're in the attic?" as he looked up, staring over his head.

Glenda said, "Yes, they are making our house better."

Tommy responded, "Up there with Shaw?"

"Yes, we are going to get him out," Glenda encouraged.

Tommy looked down while playing with a bracelet and replied, "Yater" as he tried to say later.

"He's going to leave later?" Glenda asked.

Tommy said, "Shaw can leave later,"

Glenda got freaked out and said to Bo as she just walked outside for a moment, "You're staying the night."

Meanwhile back in the attic, Chris and Harmony began round two. Chris had Harmony warn Bo downstairs things were about to begin once again. Bo walked back into the house as Glenda and Tommy remained outside.

CONNECTICUT – THE CONFRONTATION

Harmony yelled down, "We are starting, listen for anything and be alert."

Chris looked at Harmony to prepare her as she picked up the cross once more. They both knew that no matter what happened next, there was no 10-13 coming, no back up on the way.

Chris exhaled. He looked at his wife and partner as he said, "Here we go."

This time he picked up the book that contained his own prayer that he created with God. Many of the foundational prayers of the last decade which helped ground him in his relationship with his eternal Father. These were not just Biblical but personal. What the Christian faith was all about to him. All the training, all the ministry, all the time spent with God was leading up to this moment.

As soon as he started up, the mysterious sound began without hesitation. This time Bo threw on her video downstairs as Chris recorded upstairs. The roar could be heard throughout the entire house. As she could hear the faint voice of prayer upstairs two flights up in the attic, the angry roar grew louder in ferocity.

Bo looked out the window towards Glenda and Tommy. Their backs were to her as they were on the outside stairs now that the rain began to give way to the sun once again. They had no idea what was happening inside... or so she thought.

Tommy began to get antsy. He leaned backwards, twisting awkwardly like children do and looked toward the top of the house a few times.

CONNECTICUT – THE CONFRONTATION

Glenda knew he was in tune with what's happening. She witnessed too many events over the past few weeks not to know.

Glenda asked, "What's happening up there Tommy?"

Tommy replied as he was playing around, "He's hurt."

Glenda asked, "What hurt him?"

Tommy seemed to ignore the question as his attention went back to the top of the house.

He pointed up and said, "He's on daaa roof."

As Chris began to switch from reading prayer to commands of authority through Christ, things heated up in the attic. He knew Marbas was drawn out into the open now. Chris always had a theory of how a house blessing or exorcism can parallel an exorcism of a person. Just as the exorcist needs to come to the point where the demon is present in the person to expel him, the same could be done in the home that is infested.

With Marbas showing his cards, Chris began to expel the demon through the authority given to him by Jesus himself. He spoke it directly from a certain passage of scripture in English but then recited it from memory in the original Koine Greek. Chris believed since this was the exact language used during the times of Jesus, and possibly spoken by the apostles as well, it could be devastating to the entity.

CONNECTICUT – THE CONFRONTATION

As Chris continued to fire away upstairs, downstairs was heating up as well. Tommy attempted to rip Glenda's cross off her neck. Without a warning, he began to claw at her, over and over, pulling on the chain. Glenda, not knowing what was happening upstairs, was about to give it to him so he would stop.

Bo staring out the window, noticed the exchange between Tommy and Glenda. She began to bang on the window to get Glenda's attention. As Glenda turned around, Bo began to yell in a low whispery voice so as not to disturb Chris and Harmony.

"Keep it on, keep it on!" she whispered.

Upstairs, Chris felt this inner power growing as the Holy Spirit grew stronger. Fear fled the attic as courage through faith was recaptured. Chris paced back and forth as he commanded the demon out in Jesus' name.

Tommy outside with his aunt.

He said pointing straight up, "He's on the...roof!" Tommy yelled out in along drawn-out voice, "Uh oh, he's falling dowwwwn!"

Upstairs, Chris finished speaking the last command in the authority of Christ.

"I command you, in the name of the Lord Jesus Christ, depart from this home, this little boy and this family.

The room went silent. Chris and Harmony just stood there sweating profusely. They felt a positive shift to the room but remained on alert for the moment. Suddenly, a

CONNECTICUT – THE CONFRONTATION

beautiful smell rushed past Harmony's face and proceeded to fill the attic.

Harmony exclaimed, "I just felt the most refreshing breeze on my face. It smells just like beautiful roses."

Sunlight beamed into the room through the once gloomy window as her face looked as refreshed as a person that had just walked into an air-conditioned room on a hot summer day. The attic, that was once filled with the putrid smell of feces and sweltering heat was replaced by the glory and peace of God.

Downstairs, the activity ceased as well. Out on the porch, Tommy stopped his onslaught for his aunt's cross. In what seemed instantaneous, he picked up his little foam Paw Patrol bat and ball. He played on the wet front lawn, looking over to Glenda, giggling as he continually missed hitting the ball as Glenda smiled back.

Bo walked out and sat down next to Glenda. She put her arm around her sister as they both smiled with a look of relief towards each other. They had been together since this all took place. This entire experience was one that neither of them believed could be possible before April. Now, at this moment, they relished the simple peace of watching little Tommy play once again as he ran around without a worry in the world, just as a child should.

Chris finished as they both gave thanks to God. He walked over to Harmony as she put her arm around him. Chris was emotionally and physically drained. The exhausted couple packed up their gear and headed to the opening, preparing to climb down. As Chris dropped his legs into the opening to catch the ladder, he looked back to Harmony for the bag.

CONNECTICUT – THE CONFRONTATION

Chris was oblivious to what had just taken place with the family. He smiled towards Harmony with a look of relief.

He said, "At least nothing happened down there with them."

As they all met up downstairs, Glenda and Bo thanked Chris and Harmony emotionally while hugging the couple. Chris looked at Harmony as they knew something went on here during their time in the attic.

The family shared all the events that seemed to happen simultaneously with the expulsion of the demonic entity. Chris and Harmony sat down as they were trying to fill in the timeline of events. This was very big news.

Chris said, "This tells us that the prayers were having a positive effect in getting rid of this thing. He was being affected around the home and around Tommy. We won't know for sure for a couple of days, but it looks good."

Chris had a better understanding from the events that occurred that day, that Tommy was being oppressed and not possessed. Marbas was still operating outside him and influencing him, which was much different than controlling him in full possession.

This case presented the classic demonic activity in most cases right from the beginning. The haunting of a home in the first stage to the next stage of the haunting of a person in the little boy. If things continued in the direction they were heading, possession would have been the final result.

CONNECTICUT – THE CONFRONTATION

Chris and Harmony finished up the blessing by filling the entire home with frankincense and holy water. Chris anointed Glenda, Bo, and Tommy with blessed oil and prayed specific prayers over Tommy.

Now was the time to explain to the family in a little more detail what happened, and what do they do from here. He sat down across from Glenda and Bo, with his wife next to him. Glenda had set Tommy up in his bedroom with some snacks as the adults spoke.

Chris said, "What happened in your home and to your nephew was the result of an invitation to a demon."

Glenda replied, "What I don't understand is how? I would never do such a thing."

"Absolutely not," Chris responded in agreement.

"It wasn't you, it was the invitation from the prior owner, as all the evidence points to Satanic witchcraft. She performed a conjuring spell, a powerful one, even using her own blood. I believe she placed a curse here to terrorize the new owners. Especially after she could not gain access back to the home. It makes sense when you think about it."

Chris continued, "The world is made up of good and evil. This is played out through humanity. Just as someone may pray for you through God, another may curse you, calling on the devil."

Chris always told people, when someone cuts you off on the road, be careful who you give the finger to. You have no idea who that person is or what that other person practices. You may think twice about how far road rage can really go.

The women were captivated that these things really existed, let alone in her dream home turned nightmare. Chris continued, "The markings all around the attic and property were to this specific demon who manifested as a result."

Glenda was confused. She said, I heard about the devil and demons when we used to go to Church, but they never said something like this could happen."

Chris answered, "Well here is the thing, there are two types of activity. One which affects all of us is called temptation. That's probably what you have learned. That's true. That is most common. The devil will tempt each person according to his weakness. This is the time when we grow with God. It is basically a time of testing. This is where the devil unknowingly helps us get closer to God believe it or not. Without trials, tribulations, or temptations, we would never have the opportunity to see God's great power and love taking us through these moments."

He continued, "But there is another type of activity, something you just experienced, it has been called extraordinary activity. When we begin to head in a direction which chooses to abandon God and seek something else for power, this can be the result. Sometimes the individual will open this door or someone else will as in the case with the witch."

Bo chimed in and asked, "But why was Tommy affected?"

Chris replied, "That's a great question. What this entity was doing was looking for a way to stay. Demons are bullies, so he chose the weakest vessel, a little boy who has difficulty communicating. He was looking to gain continued invitations which would also help him grow in strength. So, as you witnessed, the activity amped up day after day in the home as well as Tommy having increased interaction with this thing. He was befriending him to gain rights to stay but soon after he would have attempted possession. At that time, he would have shown his true evil and it would have been a different relationship."

Harmony got up and went to sit with the women as she noticed they were still a little shaken up from the earlier events. Now understanding the truth was refreshing but something new to them. It was a lot to take in, but Chris knew that he withheld this all for good reason during the case. Now was the time to be informed to protect them.

He continued, "I'm telling you all this not to scare you but to help you. It is important for you to understand, that God saved you. Harmony and I are just messengers. None of us have any power over the demonic. His faithfulness, power and love for your family showed up to rescue you today."

"He kicked this thing clear out of here," he said with a smile.

They all laughed as the little humor was very welcoming after the horror they all just experienced.

Chris said, "I'm going to tell you, what I tell everyone after a case. We are not here to preach but to deliver the truth. It's up to you to decide. Everyone has a choice before God."

Jesus said in the scriptures,

CONNECTICUT – THE CONFRONTATION

"When an evil spirit leaves a person, it goes into the desert, seeking rest but finding none. Then it says, 'I will return to the person I came from. So, it returns and finds its former home empty, swept, and in order. Then the spirit finds seven other spirits more evil than itself, and they all enter the person and live there. And so that person is worse off than before."

Chris continued, "Look at today like this. Jesus has put your lives back in order. And amazing as that is, God showed you His power and that He is mindful of you."

When Chris said those words, he began to feel choked up. He instantly remembered the day God came through for the Africa trip.

Trying to compose himself, he looked at the women and said, "It is up to you to fill your lives with him. Change your life towards him and believe He is who He says He is."

Looking towards Harmony, he said, "Jesus changed our lives in an instant and now we are here to help you. Trust him and your life will never be the same."

They all hugged as they said their goodbyes. They knew they would all see each other again. There is a bond created in these moments that cannot be broken. God had always rewarded Chris and Harmony with one great blessing when a case had finished, family. Both, with very little family left, gained new family members that day...It was a good day!

As for the Satanic Witch of Connecticut? Weeks later, while Chris and Harmony were enjoying a Sunday

CONNECTICUT – THE CONFRONTATION

afternoon at home with the family, Chris received a call. As Chris had the phone call on speaker, one of the staff members from the newsroom who covered the Connecticut news story, told him that they just received a report of a strange woman at a nearby motel. She was leaving strange symbols on apartment doors and animal parts on their porches.

Chris hung up the phone and turned around to see that the family was listening to the call. He looked at Harmony with intrigue as they finally got a possible location on the woman. He got up and was heading over to the table to sit down for a nice family dinner. Just then, Beckie called out to her dad as if she was the spokesperson for the group.

Beckie said with a smile, "Its ok dad. We know. We'll save you some dinner."

Chris grabbed one of the black cases containing his investigating equipment, kissed them all goodbye and headed for the door. But that's another story... for another day.

TO THE READER

    I had no idea at the time that writing this book would be one of the most important decisions of my life. Since being called into ministry, or many different Ministries I should say, you can sometimes get lost to who you are, what you should be doing or even forget where you started. It was not until revisiting my life in each chapter of this book that I began to see with clarity of what God intentionally laid out for my life, step by step.

    One thing occurred as I began writing this book that I would never have expected. I experienced each emotion to the fullest as I relived not just the victories but the tragedies throughout my life. It became so bad that I had developed an illness that Harmony and I could not understand. At one point it was as if the entire left side of my body was experiencing a numbness, then a strange rash days later. After seeking medical attention, I was diagnosed with Shingles and the cause was extreme stress. So many of the chapters were met with flashbacks and tears that I had no idea that my body was manifesting the pain.

    I will say today that this experience, as painful as it might have been, was a blessing in disguise and has made the direction of my life clearer as a husband, a father and in ministry. Just as I could now see how God had determined the steps of my life from the beginning, I firmly believe that this book was just the next step of that plan.

    We live in a world of constant noise and if you don't take the time to look back sometimes and see what brought you to the place you now call the present...well, you can lose direction. The one thing to remember is that God is always in control. Through the noise, the trials and the sufferings come healing, peace, and strength. When you begin to approach these things in a positive light, you will begin to see that He just may be preparing you for something you never expected...Get ready!

***"The mind of a person plans his way, But the LORD directs his steps"* Proverbs 16:9**

I am honored and thankful that you would take the time to read my book. If you enjoyed what you read, I would be grateful if you could leave a review on Amazon.

If you have any questions, please don't hesitate to reach out to me. I could be contacted through my email at Chrisdeflorio777@gmail.com. God bless all of you.

To God be the glory,

Chris DeFlorio

ABOUT THE AUTHOR

Chris DeFlorio was a Nationally Certified Paramedic during the 90's while running an ambulance in the busy South Bronx for the New York City Fire Department. As he moved to the New York City Police Department in 2003, he spent years in the plain clothes unit as a cop at the dangerous 32 Precinct in Harlem. There he experienced every kind of evil while studying the crime habits of the city's worst and most violent offenders. He is a Christian who has worked ministry for over 15 years ranging from evangelism, caring for the homeless throughout New York to missionary work in Africa. Chris has been featured in an international Documentary called "It's Coming." As well he has been interviewed in dozens of articles ranging from Hauntings to Visionary serial killers like Ted Bundy and Lori Vallow. Now, along with his wife, he combines his first responder skills acquired over 25 years' experience and faith as they travel the country investigating and helping families with demonic issues infesting their lives.

Website: https://chrisdeflorio.com/

Notes

Notes

Notes

Notes

Notes

Made in United States
Orlando, FL
15 September 2024